# STORM

## Books by Jim Cymbala

*Breakthrough Prayer*
(book and audio)

*The Church God Blesses*
(book and audio)

*Fresh Faith*
(book and audio)

*Fresh Power*
(book and audio)

*Fresh Wind, Fresh Fire*
(book and audio)

*The Life God Blesses*
(book and audio)

*Storm*
(book and audio)

*When God's People Pray*
(book and audio)

*You Were Made for More*
(book and audio)

# JIM CYMBALA

WITH JENNIFER SCHUCHMANN

# STORM

## HEARING JESUS *for* THE TIMES WE LIVE IN

ZONDERVAN

*Storm*
Copyright © 2014 by Jim Cymbala

ISBN 978-0-310-33841-3 (ebook)

Requests for information should be addressed to:
Zondervan, 3900 *Sparks Dr., Grand Rapids, Michigan 49546*

---

Library of Congress Cataloging-in-Publication Data

Cymbala, Jim, 1943-
    Storm : hearing Jesus for the times we live in / Jim Cymbala, with Jennifer
Schuchmann.
       pages   cm
    Includes bibliographical references.
    ISBN 978-0-310-24126-3 (hardcover)
    1. United States – Church history – 21st century. 2. Christian life – United States.
 I. Title.
    BR515.C98 2014
    243 – dc23                                         2014016662

---

Published in association with the literary agency of Ann Spangler and Company, 1420 Pontiac Road S.E., Grand Rapids, MI 49506.

Cover design: Curt Diepenhorst
Cover photo: Marcos Welsh / Getty Images® royalty free
Interior design: Matthew Van Zomeren

*First Printing September 2014 / Printed in the United States of America*

# CONTENTS

## [ Chapter 1 ]

# STORM APPROACHING

Warning Signs for the Church

I sat alone in our twenty-sixth-floor apartment the night a deadly visitor arrived. My wife, Carol, was in Nashville working on a new CD project for the choir. I might have been tempted to leave town with her earlier had I known how violent my unwelcomed guest would become.

Though I had been warned of her likely appearance for hours, I wasn't too alarmed as I awaited her arrival. *How bad could it be?* Despite the strong warnings, she was only passing through New York, a stopover on her way from the Caribbean to an unknown destination off the coast of eastern Canada. I hadn't yet fully grasped the wrath she would bring or the darkness she would leave behind.

Throughout that ominous day, I had watched the thick clouds churning in the sky as the smog-diffused gray light gave way to a full moon and a wet, shadowy night. Looking out the window, I could see that the stores had closed early due to the unusual weather forecast. Below me, Brooklyn was unusually deserted. The streets were devoid of both people and cars. It was jarring to be in such a large downtown area and not see another soul.

I was lonely and called Carol.

As the night wore on, I heard the wind. It whistled through the walls and rattled the double-plated glass windows. Fifteen months earlier, Carol and I had moved from a house to this apartment. I wasn't yet familiar with how this new high rise would hold, so as the storm outside intensified, so did my anxiety. Driving rain began to pelt the windows. Winds whipped around our building, and debris launched from the streets flew several stories high. The gloomy day became a frightening night. My thoughts raced: How would the building handle what was about to be unleashed?

She blew into Brooklyn with a force I had never experienced. New Yorkers are famously tough, but we were no match for this kind of power. The local television stations reported damage in New Jersey and along the coast. Trees fell in Long Island, taking down power lines. When Sandy's punch landed exactly at high tide, she served up murky water like a busted fire hydrant. Seawater rushed into power stations and subways in Lower Manhattan. Hospitals began to evacuate the sick, sending them home or transporting them by ambulance to hospitals farther inland.

The superstorm raged, and I had no idea how deadly she was or how much destruction she left in her path. I wouldn't discover those things until the light of morning. However, that night I saw something I had never seen before. Or rather, I didn't see something I'd always seen — Lower Manhattan *disappeared* into the night. The lights that always glowed from the financial district were gone! The power that physically and metaphorically lit the world had been cut off at the source.

To a Brooklynite who uses the skyline of Manhattan to navigate, the way a cowboy uses the North Star, it was unfathomable to think that parts of New York City could just suddenly dissolve into darkness. I thought of all the wealth and influence concentrated in the financial district alone. The people who lived and worked there swayed the entire world's economy with a few keystrokes.

But now, with their power cut, the great buildings where they worked were dark. And thousands of people who labored there during the week were powerless to do anything about it. It was startling to think how such vast influence could just disappear.

During the next few days, I saw more images of Sandy's deadly devastation. Boardwalks and amusement rides had been ripped from their foundations and tossed out to sea. Houses were torn to splintered shreds of plywood, and open gas lines fed flames, causing entire neighborhoods to burn. Coastlines disappeared, and maps would forever be redrawn.

I learned how our church was personally affected. Members lost homes and vehicles. One of our keyboard players had both of his cars washed away. Sadly, up and down the East Coast many people lost their lives.

But the image I kept returning to, the one that haunted me, was the absence of light and power in Lower Manhattan. It struck me that this could be the perfect metaphor for what is happening in the Christian church today.

> **Is the light of Jesus that we are to shine before people growing dark? Has another kind of storm cut us off from *our* power source?**

Is the light of Jesus that we are to shine before people growing dark?

Has another kind of storm cut us off from *our* power source?

Is the church of Christ disappearing into a dark night?

## POWERFUL AND DEADLY STORMS

Superstorm Sandy was bad, but deadlier storms have hit our shores.

In 2008, Hurricane Katrina sent ocean water rushing over the levees, destroying parts of New Orleans, displacing millions of residents, and killing more than 1,800 people. The Galveston Hurricane of 1900 took even more lives. When the storm came inland, approximately 8,000 people who chose to ignore the warnings were swept out to sea.

Had they understood what was coming, they would have chosen differently.

However, the intensity of a storm isn't always visible at its birth. Sandy wasn't more than a blip on the radar in the Caribbean, but the right conditions quickly fueled her growth. Likewise, on December 26, 2004, sailors either didn't see or didn't pay attention to the small bulges on the water's surface. The one-foot swells were barely perceptible in the enormous Indian Ocean. But as waves reached the shallow coastlines, the sea began to rise dramatically, eventually unleashing fifty-foot waves and killing about 200,000 people. The energy released by the Indian Ocean Tsunami was estimated to be the equivalent of 23,000 Hiroshima-type atomic bombs. What started out as a one-foot wave grew to become one of the deadliest natural disasters in history.

I believe we are in the early stages of a storm that has the potential to damage our churches, our families, and ultimately the cause of Christ in the nation.

I believe followers of Jesus in America are on the cusp of something horrible. I, and many others, see the early warning signs all around. You may see them too. I want you to consider three specifically.

## WARNING NO. 1 – WE'RE NOT AS BIG AS WE THINK

A quick Google search will reveal some surprising statistics about Christians in America. For example, one website says that 246,780,000 people (79.5 percent of the population) in the United States are Christians.[1] That's a huge percentage of Americans who claim to be followers of Christ!

But is it true or a bogus number?

If nearly 80 percent of the population were Christian, wouldn't we see the effects of that in culture?

Let me ask the question in a different way. Are eight out of ten people in your school, office, or community Bible-believing, church-going followers of Jesus? That's not the case in Brooklyn, where I live and work. My guess is that's not the case where you live either.

In the book *The Great Evangelical Recession*, author John S. Dickerson takes a closer look at these often exaggerated statistics and the data behind them and finds that the numbers don't add up. He points out that the vast majority of those claiming to be "Christian" rarely attend any church, nor do they trust in Christ alone for their salvation, nor do they value God's Word as the only rule for faith and practice.

You've run into this before, right?

You're in a conversation with someone who said they were a "Christian," but as the conversation moves deeper, you find their thinking plainly non-Christian. They don't value the Bible as God's Word. Or they maintain that there are multiple ways to receive salvation and Jesus is just one of those. What they describe is so different from what you know the Bible teaches, it is hard to imagine how they could call themselves believers in Jesus.

Jenny, a friend from church, recently had a conversation with a woman who identified herself as a Christian. Yet as the conversation developed, the woman also told Jenny that she believed that everyone should make up their own religion. Perhaps they should also make up a name for that religion, because *it is not Christianity*!

To get an accurate count of Bible-believing Christians in America, Dickerson looked at four studies by four different researchers who had four different motivations and used four different methodologies to calculate the number. Their unanimous conclusion was that "the actual number of evangelical Christians is shockingly between 7 to 8.9 percent of the United States population, not 40 percent and certainly not 70 percent."[2] That's right, only 7 to 8.9 percent of America.

The truth is that the number of real believers in Jesus is in a massive decline, and that decline is happening much more rapidly than we have thought. While many boast of America being a "Christian nation," Dickerson's researchers say it's fewer than one out of ten. And it gets worse. He predicts that within thirty years, the number of evangelical Christians will drop to one in every twenty-five Americans!

These numbers are a clear warning that the lights are going out.

## WARNING NO. 2 – PERSONAL TRANSFORMATION IS RARE

Over the last decade, leaders from several denominations have told me that new members, average attendance, baptisms, and giving have all declined in their churches. The largest evangelical denomination sadly reports that new converts as measured by baptisms in 2012 was the lowest since 1948![3]

Talking with pastors throughout the country, I know these trends aren't limited to any one denomination. Recently, while in Louisiana, I prayed at an altar with a pastor who was distraught over the lack of spiritual results in his ministry. This man had been a pastor for nearly thirty years and had weathered many of the typical ups and downs pastors experience. He had a passion for ministry, and all he wanted to do was lead people to Jesus. With a heavy heart and tears in his eyes, he said, "Listen, Jim, I love God, but I haven't baptized ten new converts in two years! There are people all around who need Jesus, but I can't seem to reach them. I don't know what to do." Then he broke down sobbing.

His story isn't unique or surprising.

In 2012 the Barna Group found that 46 percent of churchgoers said "their life had not changed at all as a result of churchgoing."[4]

**More than half of churchgoers don't remember even one significant new insight gained by going to God's house! Something strange is going on here.**

On top of that, "three out of five church attenders (61 percent) said they could not remember a significant new insight gained by attending church services."[5] What is even more bothersome is that "one-third of those who have attended a church in the past have *never* felt God's presence while in a congregational setting" (emphasis added).[6]

Think of it: More than half of churchgoers don't remember even one significant new insight gained by going to God's house!

Something strange is going on here.

It is obvious the overwhelming majority of our ministries are not producing much fruit in the form of converted, changed lives. And people are not experiencing God in our churches. This would have been unthinkable in the early days of the Christian church as described in the New Testament. This is a *critical* warning sign that something is terribly wrong.

## WARNING NO. 3 – BIBLICAL LITERACY IS DECLINING

Not only are the majority not getting spiritual insight from their church experience, but a growing number aren't getting it from the Bible either. According to the American Bible Society's "State of the Bible 2013" report, the number of Americans who are antagonistic toward the Bible has increased from 10 percent to 17 percent from 2011 to 2013.[7] Where will we be in five or ten years if this trend continues?

To counter that statistic, at first glance it might seem positive that two out of three Americans believe the Bible contains everything a person needs to live a meaningful life.[8] But only one out of five (21 percent) actively read the Bible at least four times a week.[9] Even among churchgoers who believe the Bible is the inspired Word of God, *only 20 percent* say they think about it during the day.[10] God has spoken to us through his Word, but fewer are taking the time to listen.

Surveys also show that there is barely any difference between the lifestyles of Christian churchgoers and the behavior of those who don't believe in God at all. Yet the Scriptures define believers in Jesus as "saints," a people who have been separated from the world and belong exclusively to Jesus.

Fewer people inside the church believe in the truth and power found in Scripture. An even smaller percentage actively read and apply its truth to their lives. This turning away from Scripture is another calamitous sign.

## THE CHURCH IS LOSING ITS LIGHT AND POWER

We have seen this picture, right?

Adults drag themselves out of bed to attend church from a sense of duty or obligation. There is little joy in their worship or power in their prayers. Teens and young adults profess to be believers, but half of those born into the church leave it, and those who remain don't generally seem too excited about Jesus of Nazareth. The young blame the older people running the church, and the older people running the church blame the young for running away from it. Young and old can't agree on the style of music and use that as an excuse not to participate. Thankfully, there are many exceptions, but the handwriting remains on the wall.

If there are decreasing signs of spiritual life — conversions to Christ through the preaching of the gospel, growing congregations, services filled with Bible teaching, prayer, and love for one another — something must be terribly wrong. While politicians are experts at spinning uncomfortable facts, as Christians we can't afford to explain away the obvious. Our light in the world is flickering, and we must face that reality.

Some Christian leaders have sadly confessed to me that the decline is so severe among their ranks that unless something turns around, unless God visits them in a fresh way, their denomination will probably barely exist in a decade or two.

Many Christians are bewildered, disheartened, and concerned by what they see — a culture that has become increasingly hostile to biblical Christianity and a church whose vital signs are rapidly waning.

It is easier to deny these statistics than to embrace them. But calling something not true that is true doesn't change the truth. Maybe we are tempted to dismiss these warnings with empty platitudes or "faith talk" that repeatedly denies reality or declares that "God is on the throne" and "God is good all the time," as if repeating those slogans will stop the storm from sweeping across the American church.

But the decline is even worse elsewhere. For example, Scotland was once home to some of the greatest revivals, most gifted pastors, best religious writers, and strongest churches in history. Yet I recently read that the Christian church in Scotland has so declined that at the current rate the church will basically cease to exist by the year 2047.

How could this happen in Scotland? Some of the greatest missionaries in the history of Christianity were sent out into the world from there. Nevertheless, in a few years Scotland may be almost devoid of Christian witness.

Let us not be blind to the warning signs or dismiss them with a trite, "That can't happen to the Christian church in America." God certainly *is* on the throne, but this decline surely saddens his heart. We can't use "faith talk" or mental positivism to avoid the reality facing us. We must choose whether to be like the Texans in Galveston and watch the rushing waves that threaten to wipe us out, or heed the obvious warnings and act.

## DEADLY FORCES FROM OUTSIDE THE CHURCH?

One cause of our current plight is that we spend too much time complaining about forces outside of the church and seeking external solutions to internal problems. We blame the current president (or the past president) or Congress for policies we don't agree with. We fault the economy when we see a decline in church offerings, rather than accept that it's also a problem of the heart. We attempt to legislate morality through public policy rather than by seeing Christ give people a new heart.

But instead of our influence increasing as we seek political solutions, our influence has declined. We are the butt of jokes, the perceived enemy of freedom, and the recipients of the label "judgmental" by those who don't share our values. Political activism has had little effect on the nation, and worse, the spiritual temperature of our churches has suffered. Political rancor and the love of Jesus don't walk together easily.

We also blame culture. As a people who believe our lives should be different from the world, we are aware of the evils of secularism. Yet we simultaneously mimic the ways of the world in hopes of packaging our faith into "Christianity Lite" — a spiritual candy we can toss at nonbelievers rather than confronting the hostile reactions that can occur when we proclaim the real gospel of Jesus Christ. Pandering to the culture with prepackaged truth nuggets hasn't made us *more* effective; it has made us *ineffective*.

> As a people who believe our lives should be different from the world, we are aware of the evils of secularism. Yet we simultaneously mimic the ways of the world.

Superstorm Sandy was an external storm that paid a deadly visit to the East Coast, and we likewise want to shift the focus to outside influences. Politicians. Media. Athletes and Hollywood. The young. The old. The list of targets is pretty creative. But nowhere in the New Testament do we see the early church discussing any of that. No, they went about doing what God told them to do, continually seeking the Lord for his blessing, regardless of what political or cultural storms raged around them. That was their secret to effectiveness: They focused on the simple instructions Christ gave them and expected his grace to help them.

Many devoted Christians see the warning signs and recognize our failed attempts to turn back the tide. They know the current trends are sure signs that a spiritual storm is upon us. They are frustrated with church services that are shallow and powerless, but they don't want to come across as critical or super spiritual. They see few converts made and are increasingly concerned about their own children's relationship with the Lord. While our culture rapidly deteriorates, they aren't fooled by the hype in some religious quarters, nor the "Don't worry, God is sovereign!" attitude of others who have their heads in the sand. They see the effects of the storm tearing at their families and communities. Most of all, they know it's impossible for any nation to change unless we Christians and our churches become the spiritual light and salt of which Jesus spoke.

Regardless of where we are in the storm — beginning, middle, or end — God hasn't asked us to take shelter under a table while the light and power go out of his church. No, God has given us the gospel of Christ and the Holy Spirit's resources to help us bring light into a dark world. He sent Jesus to calm the winds, and it was Jesus who called Peter to walk with him on water. We are called to join Jesus in his work, to let our light shine in the darkness.

There is an answer to this ominous, gradual moral decline in the church of Christ. I believe that the God who loves us and sent his Son to die on a cross for us will respond to our call for help during this storm. I believe he will show us what is wrong with our thinking and grant us the answers we seek. In this book I hope to point out some of the areas I feel he has shown me. I also want to introduce you to some people who have weathered their own personal storms and demonstrate how Jesus has helped their light to shine even in abject darkness.

Together, I hope these things will light a path back to the New Testament church, where the gospel was shared with power and persecuted believers "were filled with joy and with the Holy Spirit" (Acts 13:52).

God is certainly not being glorified in the declining numbers of converts and loss of spiritual fervency among his people. This is not his purpose for us any more than the lukewarmness of the church at Laodicea, which, in love, he openly rebuked (Rev. 3:14 – 22). For them, as with us, he is standing at the door knocking and waiting for our response. If we humble ourselves and admit failing him, will he not compassionately draw near to us with mercy and grace?

Unlike Lower Manhattan during Superstorm Sandy, we must not disappear into the darkness of the storm. We are the light of the world, and we have God's message of Christ to proclaim and his promise to help us shine our light through the blackest night. The question is, are we willing to honestly assess our position in the storm and look to God to guide us through it?

# Chapter 2

# TEMPEST WITHIN

## The Failure of Church Fads and Trends

"Carmen" was a devoted Christian and a mature woman of faith. While visiting Brooklyn, she asked for a counseling appointment, but I initially declined, since I learned that Carmen worked for the pastor of her church. I didn't think counseling another pastor's member and employee was the wisest choice for me.

"Please!" she begged. "I need an objective read on something, and I think you may be the one who can help me."

I reluctantly agreed.

Carmen visited Brooklyn, and we met in my office, where she spilled out her story. "I have been working at a church for almost twenty years. My pastor is a good man whom I love and respect, but I can't take it anymore. I'm so discouraged and disillusioned, I don't even want to go to church sometimes."

She explained that for the past decade, the church had been in a lull with sagging attendance, decreasing contributions, few converts, and little enthusiasm among the congregation.

"Some years ago, our pastor announced a new day was dawning for our church. Our staff and leadership were sent to visit a mega-church out west where they learned the latest techniques the mega-church was using to increase their attendance. The leaders there

17

predicted we could have the same numerical success if we followed their strategic plan. We purchased the required books and training videos so we could come back and cast the same vision to our congregation."

Carmen described how the techniques were implemented, only to find that after two-to-three years of the "new vision," things had gone farther south. The spiritual apathy, declining attendance, and lack of new believers in Jesus continued. By now, the congregation was quietly wondering what happened to the new vision. The staff tiptoed around the subject, because what was supposed to be the "answer" hadn't made any difference at all.

"We've been slowly plodding along until a few months ago when our leaders excitedly announced they had found 'a new and better vision' for our problems," Carmen said.

The leadership team and staff went off to a conference at another megachurch, this time in the Midwest. "While there, we learned *their* formula for success. We bought more materials and came home to cast yet another vision to the congregation. The difference was that this time it was recommended we make two practical changes right from the start."

"What kind of changes?" I asked.

"They felt it would be great to paint the auditorium a different color and install thousands of dollars' worth of new lights to bring a different vibe in the room."

Amazing! No wonder churches like Carmen's remain stagnant and lifeless. How can any "formula" ever bring spiritual change if not accompanied by God's power and blessing? The pastor never even seemed to think of calling the congregation to prayer and to ask for God's help. Nor was the Holy Spirit asked for insight into the spiritual causes of the lethargy in the church. Furthermore, the leadership probably never thought to analyze whether they were actually proclaiming the powerful gospel of Jesus Christ as the apostles did. Instead, they focused on stylistic, surface recommendations such as paint colors and lights from church growth consultants.

**How can any "formula" ever bring spiritual change if not accompanied by God's power and blessing?**

Of course Carmen felt discouraged!

Although her church is orthodox in doctrine and believes in the Bible, it seems that Christ's way to build his church was ignored. This dear sister and her husband knew both God and their Bible. They also realized that cosmetic solutions to spiritual problems are never the answer.

I sympathized with her and understood their discouragement.

But I also sympathized with the pastor. Years of stagnation would be hard for anyone in the ministry to endure. I wondered how many other options he had explored and how desperate he must have become to think that paint and light fixtures might solve their problems.

Carmen and I finished our conversation, and I did my best to advise her. Together we prayed for God to direct her and her family in regard to God's will for them in the future.

## MODERN TRENDS WILL ALWAYS MISS THE POINT (AND DISAPPOINT)

Carmen's experience isn't unique. I have heard similar stories from numerous discouraged pastors who have spent a decade or more following the latest church fads and trends with lackluster results. As a result of this tempest within the church, many of these pastors feel so hopeless that if they could get a job outside of the church, they would leave the ministry altogether.

I was born and raised in New York City, and I have pastored in downtown Brooklyn for decades. It's obvious what's going on outside the walls of our churches. We are seeing a new in-your-face ungodliness. People are passing daily into eternity without Christ and couldn't seem to care less. Christian young people head to college and often lose their faith before their sophomore year. Oxycodone, cocaine, and other drugs are destroying lives no matter the economic strata. Shattered marriages result in broken homes and children raising themselves. And the freedom to preach and practice the truth of the Bible is ever so slowly eroding before our eyes.

In the midst of all this, are these so-called experts really discussing changing the lights and wall color? It takes my breath away. What world are people living in, and what Bible are they reading?

I am not a reactionary. If relaxing colors and new lighting make for a better experience inside the church, then go for it. I think there is value in paying attention to the environment where we worship, preach, and teach, and I will support whatever wall color and theatrical lights you want to use. But if we really believe surface stylistic changes are the answer for a dying church, we are out of touch with God and grieving the Holy Spirit. It's as if God never said, "Call on me in the day of trouble; I will deliver you, and you will honor me" (Ps. 50:15). And it's as if Jesus never promised, "But you will receive power when the Holy Spirit comes on you; and you will be my witnesses" (Acts 1:8).

In this book I am not trying to be negative or hypercritical. I am a minister of the gospel who loves the body of Christ. But I have watched as the pendulum has swung so far in the direction of perpetually "reinventing" ourselves that we have ended up largely ignoring God's timeless answers. Consider some of the models being followed today and ask yourself if this is God's answer for the spiritual needs of a world Christ died for.

### The Entertainment Church

The goal of this model is to fill up the church seats on Sunday. Spiritual content is secondary. To accomplish this goal, the church labors to put on the best show in town. Churches that follow this model tend to cut out all the parts of a service that don't seem exciting and entertaining. You will recognize this church model not only by their seeker-sensitive mission statement, but often by their preoccupation with staging, creative lighting, and visuals. Their aim often seems more to create a "club feel" than inviting the presence of God. Even the praise and worship element is usually more like a concert or spectator event rather than the whole congregation worshiping the Lord from their hearts.

Leaders of these churches will say their goal is to attract unbelievers and to keep them coming back until they fall in love with Jesus. But often the message they are preaching is so watered down that attendees rarely get confronted with the true gospel of Jesus Christ.

Some pastors who follow the entertainment model of church secretly fear that preaching about repentance and the death of Christ for sin might become a hindrance to getting people to come back next week. If Jesus is preached at all, it is often a "Gospel Lite" message that ignores the confrontational parts of Scripture. But without preaching the gospel found in the Bible, without a call to repent from sin and believe in the Lord Jesus Christ, and without an explanation of the blood of Christ and the new life God has offered, how will anybody be forgiven and have their life transformed? Aren't changed lives the only thing that matters to God? Or is it church attendance numbers?

Leaders who follow this model don't point so much to the testimonies of individuals radically changed by Jesus, but rather to the size of the crowd. They think they are succeeding when their numbers grow, with little thought of spiritual quality. Unfortunately, the church can become a revolving door where people stay until they get tired of the show, then leave, and don't come back.

But for two thousand years, the goal of Christianity has never been putting on a great show. Not only has the result of our preoccupation with numerical growth weakened us spiritually, but amazingly, the percentage of Christians is dramatically decreasing! Nowhere in the Bible do we see examples of Christ followers watering down or holding back parts of the message in order to hold the crowd. They preached the gospel with power and let God take care of the numbers.

As pastors and church leaders, we are never called by God to build large churches. Rather, he tells us to be faithful in preaching the truth as it is in Jesus. Of course, when we preach the gospel, *not everyone* repents and believes. But when we ignore the gospel in favor of shallow religious talk, we hurt the cause of Christ.

### Relevant Church

This model acts as if biblical truth isn't relevant for the contemporary mind; therefore, it is the pastor's top priority to preach in a style that will relate to the audience. While it is important to help people understand the content of a message, the truth we are sharing must be the Christian message as found in Scripture. Unfortunately, in many quarters relevancy has become an idol to be worshiped rather than Jesus himself. Church names and their "branding" are often more highly marketed than the name of our Savior. And being hip and relevant is more important than the two-thousand-year-old gospel of Christ declared in the power of the Spirit.

I recently read a magazine article in which a pastor justified his regular use of profanity in the pulpit by saying it was his way of relating to unchurched folks. He had no problem dropping the F-bomb, because he wanted to be real and felt it would connect more effectively with those listening to him.

Of course, this is nothing more than a cheap way to get a reaction out of people. It is no different than what some radio personalities do during their drive-time shows, pushing the envelope to greater vulgarity or some off-color subject to attract listeners. People have always used filthy language, but can anyone imagine the apostle Paul using such ridiculous tactics? This is not what the apostles of Christ ever did. Making things relevant is good, but let's follow the apostles' example, assisted by the Holy Spirit's power, of also preaching the cross of Christ.

**Making things relevant is good, but let's follow the apostles' example, assisted by the Holy Spirit's power, of also preaching the cross of Christ.**

## Corporate Church

While churches should be the best-managed and most financially accountable institutions in the nation, we have gone too far when pastors try to run their churches like a Fortune 500 corporation. Instead of following the apostle Paul or other New Testament luminaries, this new model encourages the pastor to emulate a famous CEO in a high-profile American corporation. This concept is extolled at leadership conferences where business efficiency and technological innovation are emphasized more than bearing spiritual fruit that will last for eternity. Many pastors, I'm afraid, admire a Steve Jobs more than an apostle Paul.

Granted, we can learn from anybody, but to have nonbelievers who know nothing of the Holy Spirit teach church leaders how to lead Christ's church means we have lost faith in God, his Word, and his Spirit.

"But we have to be smarter and more efficient," attendees say.

Yet we also have to be careful that we are not choosing the wisdom of humans over the wisdom of God. A classic example of this is the emphasis on finding your vision for the church. This concept has been borrowed from corporate business plans (not the Bible) and sold to us as a tool to help churches grow. I believe it has done untold harm. Often the resulting vision clearly contradicts *God's* purpose for *his* church. Too many churches end up leaning on the rotten beams and tottering walls of their own human thinking. They won't hold us up, and God won't support us when we lean on them.

When I am asked what my vision for the Brooklyn Tabernacle is, I always respond, "I don't have one. Last time I read my Bible, it said it was Christ's church, not mine."

We don't need systems, strategies, and five-year business plans as much as we need to be helped by the Holy Spirit to proclaim Jesus. Our strength is not in a great marketing department, technology, or cleverly formed target groups.

How presumptuous would it be for me to have a vision for someone else's church? It wasn't I who shed blood for the people at our church; it was Jesus who went to the cross. He said he would build *his* church and the gates of Hades would not overcome it (Matt. 16:18). Notice that he didn't say he would build *our* church; nor that *we* would build his church. No, Jesus said *he* would build *his* church, using us as his instruments. We all have different church personalities, but the plan or vision belongs to Christ and is outlined in the New Testament.

We would do better simply to draw closer to Christ. Jesus said every tree is known by its fruit (Matt. 7:15–20). If these business principles are so helpful, then where is the abundant spiritual fruit? Why aren't we seeing more lives radically transformed by Christ? Why is the church in such a sad decline?

Ministers who become CEOs end up producing little, if any, spiritual fruit. They are also susceptible to ego trips and early burnout as they attempt to do God's work by relying on their own talent and cleverness. Today the church of Jesus Christ desperately needs leaders who will return to the timeless paths of eternal truth that God has always honored and blessed. That is what happened during the Reformation. Martin Luther went back to God's ageless truth in order to move the church forward. In the entire history of the Christian church, when have believers ever sought God's plan and power when it didn't bring renewal and spiritual fruit?

## Latest Faith-Fad Church

Every two-to-three years, a new "discovery" is made on how to reinvent the church. It is odd to me why, if these ideas are so great, they have such a short life span. Following the latest fad as found in a bestselling book isn't the answer unless we also receive fresh grace from God. Everything hinges on having more of Jesus.

Some years ago, a pastor whom I hold in high regard and who is an excellent man of God spoke at our Tuesday night prayer meeting about his recent book. He shared how he went into the ministry, then got desperate and had something like a "filling of the Holy Spirit" or "an encounter with Jesus" (his words), then how God subsequently blessed his church, and how his bestselling book came to be written.

Later in my office, I said, "Your talk tonight was such a blessing! But just a suggestion from a friend — I think in your next book or future talks you should emphasize more of what you said tonight about your *personal* story. I've met many people who hit a dead end after reading your book."

He asked what I meant. I explained how I had heard people talking about the methods he outlined in his book, and when they tried to imitate them, they didn't get the results they expected. I said,

> "Many people who pick up your book are looking for a formula, but what you told us tonight is that you *were looking for God*. You had a personal encounter with our Lord, and he was the one who led you down the path you outlined in your book. I think people are forgetting that part. Instead, they're focusing mainly on the *formula*. They think if they do what you did, they'll have the same results. But you experienced a personal spiritual renewal and then God led you in a specific way. He may or may not lead them the same way. They can't just plug in your techniques and, presto, get your results."

The author agreed with me. And while I know it wasn't his intention, I can't help wondering how many people bought his book, failed in following the plan, and then became discouraged with the results. Maybe Christ had another road for them to follow if they had only waited for his direction.

## Radical Church

Have you noticed the trend in some popular Christian books calling people to various forms of radical Christian commitment? While that seems like a good thing, it can easily become a new form of legalism and self-effort unless it drives us to Christ in faith. The message goes like this: Jesus said to the rich young ruler, "If you want to be perfect, go, sell your possessions and give to the poor, and you will have treasure in heaven. Then come, follow me" (Matt. 19:21). *So, listen up everybody. Are you really a Christian? Are you radical enough to give away everything you have? If not, you're not a true believer. How about moving tonight to Ethiopia and sleeping on a mat! If you've not totally sold out, you're just a make-believe Christian.*

**Christian books and Bible teachers can be helpful and inspirational, but nothing is more powerful than the living Holy Spirit working in our lives and in our churches.**

Suddenly, folks who were sure they were believers in Jesus now question their faith. Are they really sold out like the preacher said you have to be to belong to Christ? Would I move to Ethiopia tonight? If not, I'm not radical enough to be counted a Christian.

Christian books and Bible teachers can be helpful and inspirational, but nothing is more powerful than the living Holy Spirit working in our lives and in our churches. His power is not secured through following a new gospel, but only through faith and prayer. The apostles called men and women to simple faith in Christ and dependence on the Holy Spirit. Once the Lord dwells within our hearts, he alone begins the work of making us willing and able to "sell-out" to his purposes for us.

We have to be careful in receiving the latest "revelation" or teaching or fad. There will be more Christlikeness in us only when we humble ourselves and say, "God, I can't live the life you meant for me on my own. I don't have the love, wisdom, or power. But come, Holy Spirit, and pour it into me. Teach me what it means to walk in the Spirit."

### The Anti-Model: Stagnant Orthodoxy Church

In reaction to some of these new models, some mainline churches have dug their heels in and refused almost any change. "This is always the way we've done it!" they proudly exclaim as their members age and their numbers dwindle. Their services often contain nothing but dry orthodoxy, while the attendees exhibit little passion for Christ. This is a turnoff to both the younger generation and older folks who are hungry for the living God.

Orthodox theology is vital, but without the Holy Spirit's presence, services become lifeless and routine. Visitors find church boring. Hungry believers don't see signs of God's blessing or sense his touch. The service becomes an experience only for the intellect, not for the heart, and it is endured through obligation, not joy. I am not espousing emotional fanaticism, but shouldn't we fervently seek the reality of the same Holy Spirit as experienced in the New Testament church?

No one loves to study the Bible more than I do, but when we emphasize theology and doctrine *about* God over the *living* person of Jesus Christ, it quickly becomes very heady. In addition, mere theological positions can leave us powerless, while a hurting world needs Spirit-filled believers fervent for Jesus. We may have sound doctrine, but with little fellowship with the Lord, our hearts quickly grow cold. Notice how few converts are made in churches where there is little emphasis on the *living* Christ.

The only remedy is to invite Jesus in a new way into our midst.

It seems to me that with all of these new models of doing church, we are in danger of becoming like the proud Babylonians of the Old Testament whom the prophet Habakkuk described: "The wicked foe pulls all of them up with hooks, he catches them in his net, he gathers them up in his dragnet; and so he rejoices and is glad. *Therefore he sacrifices to his net and burns incense to his dragnet*" (Hab. 1:15 – 16).

Instead of honoring God, the fisherman offers worship sacrifices to his net and burns incense to his dragnet. The methods and the tools of the trade are honored more than the Almighty, who alone grants victories and provides all that we have.

The idea that a church's methods and techniques can even be mentioned in the same sentence with the gospel of Christ is a tragedy. The exaltation of church growth formulas or denominational names over the power of the Holy Spirit is deeply distressing, and we are no better than the Babylonians making sacrifices to the tools of our trade.

## ICING, BUT NO CAKE

Here is the critical question: What if the things sold to us as solutions over the past two decades — "we've got the answer" conferences, leadership books, high-profile pastors with big personalities, and new models of doing church — are really the *problem* and not the answer?

While there are some excellent churches doing great work, on the whole we are not seeing anywhere near the fruit in our churches that we read about in the New Testament. Millions of American Christians *know* deep inside that something is missing among us despite arguments and hype to the contrary.

Could it be that we have departed from eternal truth and bought into trendy concepts that in two or three years will prove to be failures?

In the last twenty years there have been more conferences and more books published on church growth than in all the prior history of our country. As new models of how to grow your church have increased in popularity, we have actually witnessed a precipitous decline of Christianity in America. The numbers are irrefutable.

So, if all these ideas are so great, why are we here?

How is it we are going backward while still clinging to every new thing coming down the pike? Maybe they are the very thing pulling us down.

I have traveled extensively and have talked to many pastors. They say, "Look, I've tried a few of these approaches, and they don't work." Then they conclude, "Maybe I'm not cut out for this." My heart goes out to these discouraged men of God. I want them to see the reason behind their discouragement. Much of what the so-called experts have been selling us is flat-out wrong. First, many of the techniques are not found in Scripture. We don't need more technicians; we simply need more of God. For two thousand years, Christianity has grown when Spirit-empowered people spread the gospel. You would think some of us might wake up and say, "Maybe our methods and new message are grieving God instead of honoring him."

Before we buy into something, we should pause to examine what it produces. If congregations are mainly prayerless and show little hunger for God's Word or his presence, why would we want to make that a new paradigm? Why would we want any solution that doesn't emulate the church Jesus began in the book of Acts?

Consider this: The country that has the fastest-growing Christian population in the world isn't following any of these models, implementing any of these programs, or reading any of these books. They can't, because in China the Christians have to mostly meet in secret! If they are able to see God's blessing in the midst of an atheistic society without all of our resources, doesn't that tell us something? And look at the brave, devoted followers of Christ God is producing there!

I am all for finding every wise way to communicate and help people understand the Word of God, but what we are talking about here is the icing — without any cake.

Isn't it evident we need more God and fewer gimmicks?

Our problem is not with a godless, secular America, but with a church that is increasingly prayerless, compromised, demoralized, and weak. We have drifted away from the Word of God and the power of the Holy Spirit.

**God's answers for us have been replaced by human intelligence, leaving us as dim lights in an increasingly dark world.**

Where will we find the grace to change? To turn things around?

When will we be desperate enough to come to God just as we are, pleading for his help and ready to follow wherever he leads?

In many places now, it seems we would rather blame the culture, the school system, the government, and the media rather than examine our own spiritual condition.

Let's be contemporary and let's be current, but let's also be anchored on Christ and his Word. Instead of "reinventing" ourselves, maybe we should *rediscover* God's plan for his church. Instead of depending on our limited IQs and concepts of clever marketing, let's humble ourselves and say, "Come, Holy Spirit, and bless in a new way the work we do for Jesus."

It is likely we are seeing a fulfillment of those perilous times that Paul told Timothy about when men would have a form of godliness, but deny its power. The Weymouth New Testament puts it this way: "(They) ... will keep up a make-believe of piety and yet live in defiance of its power" (2 Tim. 3:5).[11] Isn't that us today?

That's why our churches are so often powerless and Christianity is in decline. God's answers for us have been replaced by human intelligence, leaving us as dim lights in an increasingly dark world.

## ANOTHER NATION IN DECLINE

The current state of affairs reminds me of the book of Judges. Of all the books of the Old Testament, none is sadder to read than that one.

The "glory days" of Moses and Joshua are over, and we see Israel, God's people, at possibly their lowest spiritual point. Allegiance to God is rare, and most people seem to have forgotten him.

After Joshua's death, some in Israel took this as an opportunity to engage in idolatry and immorality, which angered God. "In his anger against Israel the LORD gave them into the hands of raiders who plundered them. He sold them into the hands of their enemies all around, whom they were no longer able to resist" (Judg. 2:14). So begins what will become seven cycles of sin and judgment, followed by the Israelites crying out for God to deliver them.

Were they Israelites?

Were they circumcised?

Were they God's covenant people?

The answer to all three questions is yes. This was happening, not to a pagan nation, but to Israel – *God's people*.

At the end of Judges, it says, "... everyone did as they saw fit" (Judg. 21:25).

Individualism expressing itself in rejection of all authority, human and divine, swept through the nation. As they turned away from God's rule, they ended up subjugated to pagan nations. Sometimes decades of slavery followed with no hope in sight. The Israelites were only delivered after they called out to God in desperation.

Then God saved them.

## WE CAN'T SAVE OURSELVES

We need God.

We all need to repent of trying to extend his kingdom in our own strength. We need *him* to change things. The great news is that he delights in helping us when we listen, trust, and obey him.

Don't we want to make a difference and see God turn around the decline in Christianity? Don't we want to see our family members and friends find Jesus as Savior? Then let's draw closer to God and talk with him. This is what sincere believers in Christ have done for hundreds of years.

And when they have, miracles happened.

Nowhere in the Bible did God ever promise that anything would "work," except him. If you're a Christian who is bewildered and disheartened by the things you see going on, or if you're a pastor or church leader who is discouraged by a lukewarm church and lack of fruit, be sure of this promise: "Come near to God and he will come near to you" (James 4:8). Let's see God do this!

# Chapter 3

# STORMING HEAVEN

The Power of Desperate Prayer

One Tuesday, while kneeling in my usual spot during our noon prayer meeting, I heard a woman's voice to my left. Her head was in her hands, and she was praying softly. But something about the *way* she prayed caught my attention. She was talking to God as if he stood five feet away.

"You know, Lord, I'm going to lose that boy to the world," she prayed through tears. She started quietly at first, but as her pleading grew stronger, her voice became louder. "I'm going to lose him to the gangs unless you come and help me. I can't do it by myself." I could hear the desperation in her prayer. She cried out to God with all the urgency of a heartbroken mom.

"You've got to do something, God! You've got to do something now!"

I could hear everything she said.

"You know his father is dead and gone," she reasoned.

There was a pause, and although I couldn't see her face, I could hear her weeping. "I'm all alone trying to raise him. And you know all the voices out there calling to him. God, you have to help me!" Her tone was so bold, sincere, heartfelt, and intimate. "If you don't help me, no one can!" she prayed, before her words dissolved into sobs.

Her prayer moved me deeply. I reached over and put my hand on her heaving shoulder and joined her in intercession for her son.

Someone once said the most awesome thing in the world is when a mere human being prays to the Creator of the universe and is heard. I felt that awe as I listened to this woman, in equal parts confidence and desperation, lift her heart up to God and pour out her soul. It was like watching one of the Psalmists crying out for help. When someone prays boldly and desperately like this, an old church catchphrase describes it as "storming heaven."

I have heard lots of prayers like hers at my church, and they have always moved me. How much more must they move our Father in heaven, who loves us dearly! Desperate and soul-stirring prayers like hers result in answers. When God is sought in desperation, he responds.

Even in hopeless situations.

## HANNAH'S PRAYER

After the dark period described in the Old Testament book of Judges, Israel's desperate situation began to turn around with the prayer of a woman named Hannah. She had had enough and decided she could not take it any longer.

Hannah was one of two wives married to a man named Elkanah. The other wife had children, but Hannah was barren. According to the Bible, Peninnah, the rival wife, would mock Hannah and make fun of her, "provoking her in order to irritate her" because "the LORD had closed Hannah's womb" (1 Sam. 1:6). Day after day, year after year, Hannah was teased and taunted, mocked and ridiculed.

Every year Elkanah's family went to the tabernacle of the Lord in Shiloh, which was the center of worship in Israel. There the family would offer sacrifices to the Lord. But that's also when Peninnah's taunting of Hannah increased, to the point where Hannah wept so hard she could no longer eat (vv. 3–8).

Each year this pattern repeated. Her husband, Elkanah, loved Hannah and gave her extra portions of the sacrifice, but that didn't heal his wife's pain. "Why don't you eat? Why are you downhearted?" he would ask Hannah. "Don't I mean more to you than ten sons?" (v. 8).

Then one year, something snapped inside of Hannah, and she suddenly refused to endure the taunts of Peninnah and accept her childless status. "*Once* when they had finished eating and drinking in Shiloh, Hannah *stood up*" (v. 9). Hannah left the table and went to pray near the doorpost of the tabernacle. It was a moment with historic ramifications.

"In her deep anguish Hannah prayed *to the LORD*, weeping bitterly" (v. 10). She didn't recite mental prayers as we often do; her *heart* went out to the Lord. Amid the backslidden and even corrupt religious establishment of that day, we see a desperate, simple woman stirred to pray a prayer that will usher in a new day in Israel's history. In her prayer she promised God that if he gave her a son, she would dedicate him to the Lord for as long as he lived. When she finished praying, she got something to eat, and her face was no longer downcast (v. 18).

It was as if she knew something was about to change.

Hannah's prayer must have been a lot like that woman's prayer I overheard that Tuesday at church. Both of these women bared their deepest desires to the Lord, and they did so with such passion! God responds to that kind of praying.

The next morning Elkanah's family arose and worshiped God before they headed back home to Ramah. Once there, Elkanah made love to his wife as he had so often done before, but this time "the LORD remembered her" (v. 19).

Hannah became pregnant and gave birth to a son.

Now, what was it that stirred Hannah to pray a prayer that changed the future of Israel?

Hannah could have chosen to live in denial. When Peninnah mocked her, she could have said, "Who cares? I'm not into kids. I don't want to change diapers anyway!" But she didn't. She faced the truth (as painful as it was), saying, "I want a baby, I want a son, I want to be fruitful."

Hannah could have forgotten her heartache and just rejoiced in the fact that she was a child of Abraham, Isaac, and Jacob and a part of the covenant people of Israel. Or she could have looked at her situation and said, "I don't have a child, so it must be God's sovereign will that I don't."

But she didn't do either of those things. Hannah's story shows us that she did not deny her barrenness, but neither did she accept it. Her unique prayer became the channel that God both prompted and then used to turn the tide in Israel and bring much-needed blessing upon them. The lesson is clear for us today. We must not silently accept *our* lack of fruitfulness and somehow justify it as God's will for us.

Imagine if Hannah had said, "Well, I guess I'm not supposed to have a baby."

No, as hard as it was, she honestly faced her circumstances and then desperately prayed for God to change them.

What was in her mighty prayer that God could not ignore?

None of us totally understands the power of prayer, but we know that Hannah's prayer was powerful and effective, the kind James describes in his epistle (James 5:16). Yet if I had to guess, I would say it was both the heightened element of desperation coupled with deep faith in God. Hannah had no other place to turn. It was as if, in her great anguish and grief, she cried, "Make me fruitful, or I don't want to go on." She was at her end. "Give me a child or I will die!"

> **We must not silently accept *our* lack of fruitfulness and somehow justify it as God's will for us.**

God heard Hannah's weeping, and her prayer became the pathway to divine intervention. Furthermore, God wanted her story told in detail in the Bible, so future generations would recognize that Israel's turnaround started with a lonely, heartbroken woman who just wanted to bear fruit.

I understand a little of that desperation to bear fruit. I have felt it myself.

## MY DESPERATE PRAYER

I remember a dark day about forty years ago when we were in our first year of ministry. I was at our church, which at the time was located in a little building on Atlantic Avenue in downtown Brooklyn. It was such a depressing time for me and for the church. We had maybe fifteen to twenty people attending regularly. The first Sunday offering was $85, and my salary was $3,800 that first year because that's all the church could afford. Carol and I were both working second jobs to make ends meet and to provide for our daughter, Chrissy.

The church building was dilapidated, and the area was overrun with heroin users, their paraphernalia often littering the sidewalks. The church was in crisis. My sermons were so bad that *I* fell asleep preaching them. Some days Carol and I didn't even want to go to church, which was a real problem, since I was in charge!

One Tuesday afternoon I began to pace back and forth at the altar area in the sanctuary. I had been pastoring for six months, and no one was finding Christ. No lives were being changed. Not *one*. If we were fortunate, there would be maybe five people coming to that night's service. I felt like a failure. This is not what I saw in Acts, where believers prayed and conversions abounded. If this is what the rest of my life held, I couldn't see the point in continuing.

I felt inadequate and blamed myself.

Many of my peers had seminary degrees. But my background was in *basketball*. When I was in college, I was the captain of the University of Rhode Island basketball team. I didn't know how to "do" church. I felt overwhelmed and deeply discouraged.

In basketball, you always knew how you were doing. A scoreboard showed whether you were winning or losing and by how much. Inside of me was this competitive edge (which, I believe, God sanctified for his glory) that wanted to win for Christ, but how was I supposed to do that?

I wasn't competing against any other church or any other pastor. I was competing against the world, the flesh, and the devil. And I felt as if I was losing. To me, the scoreboard was outside the front door of the church, where there were alcoholics and addicts sometimes propped up against our building. Young people in gangs gathered nearby, heading nowhere and messing up their lives. Marriages were deteriorating and families falling apart. Single mothers burdened with overwhelming financial and spiritual needs passed by our doors every day.

I couldn't stand the thought of not seeing a breakthrough so we could make a difference for Jesus.

"God, how could you call me to be a failure?" I asked him repeatedly that afternoon.

*Christ is the answer these people need, and I must get them to believe the gospel. Their lives can be transformed.*

*But how can I do it?*

Thoughts raced through my mind as I prayed.

*We have the gospel of Christ.*
*The Lord is with us.*

I thought of the powerful promises that had been trusted in throughout two thousand years of church history.

*"And surely I am with you always, to the very end of the age"* (Matt. 28:20).

*"But you will receive power when the Holy Spirit comes on you; and you will be my witnesses in Jerusalem, and in all Judea and Samaria, and to the ends of the earth"* (Acts 1:8).

Yet, contrasted with God's power, I had to live with Jim Cymbala's impotence and weakness, and that very thought was crushing my soul.

That afternoon as I poured out my soul to God, I battled with my lack of ability and not knowing what to do. If things were going to change, they had to start with me.

Alone in the building, I fell prostrate on the carpet and wept and prayed. I couldn't stand the thought of just holding the fort, of not experiencing the kinds of things I read of in the Bible. I wanted a personal and church revival like some of those throughout church history. I couldn't bear the thought of a fruitless life.

*God, if you're not going to change me, if you're not going to make me effective, if I'm not going to make a difference in people's lives, then I don't want to do this. What's the point of living a life that's not fruitful?*

I was so desperate that I started praying a Hannah-like prayer. As I continued, I'm not even sure how the words formed in my mind, but as I said them, I knew they came from my heart. *God, change me and use me. Let me see a breakthrough, or take my life! I don't want to live!*

With God as my witness, I meant it with all my heart! I had no doubt that God would take care of Carol and Chrissy, but I couldn't bear the thought of living in the frustration of not seeing the power of the gospel change lives as I knew it had in the past.

Forget the Brooklyn Tabernacle. The church didn't have any name recognition then. I had no "pastoral image" I was trying to uphold; I wasn't trying to build a church with large numbers or a famous choir, so I could write books or whatever. Those weren't even thoughts in my mind. At that time, as far as anyone knew, we didn't exist. We were just a sign on the outside of a decrepit building.

This was an inner primal cry — the Holy Spirit helping me pray with groans too deep to be uttered. The thought of presiding over just another ineffective church that had little or no effect on the community was more than I could bear.

I wish I could say a thousand people showed up that night and I no longer despaired, but that's not what happened. I continued to doubt my background and whether or not I would ever be effective. But something was birthed by that prayer. God saw my desperate plea and had mercy on me, because he knew that even with all my faults (many of which I still have today), I wanted to be used by him. And I wanted to see Jesus Christ get the glory.

**Why are we so slow to cry out to God when we're barren as Hannah was? Are we too proud and sophisticated to beg him for fruit?**

Name any church, anyplace, at any time, where believers got desperate and began to pray and didn't see God respond. Hasn't God always sent help from heaven to revive his people? Doesn't he want to see his kingdom extended, the prodigal come back, and families healed?

Yet why are we so slow to cry out to God when we're barren as Hannah was? Are we too proud and sophisticated to beg him for fruit?

It must be that many leaders today are either ignorant of the Bible or have never personally experienced the power of prayer and the Spirit of God. The coldest, hardest situations have been turned around by God, not because people got smarter or had more technology on hand, but because God responded somehow, some way to their prayers.

I think many Christians come to a place where either they have a breakthrough moment that brings a new chapter into their lives, or they slowly acquiesce and accept the status quo. I also feel many churches either pray down heaven's blessing or gradually turn to shallow formulaic methods instead of the living God. But we shouldn't give up or look for shortcuts. We should be like Paul, who writes in Galatians 4:19, "I travail like a mother giving birth *until* Christ be formed in you" (KJV paraphrased). The apostle certainly didn't accept the "what is"; rather, he fought for the "what could be."

Hannah also travailed, and she bore fruit.

"So in the course of time Hannah became pregnant and gave birth to a son. She named him Samuel [which sounds like the Hebrew for *heard of God*], saying, 'Because I asked the LORD for him'" (1 Sam.

1:20). The baby named Samuel was born because Hannah asked the Lord for him. God remembered her and her prayers.

We know from her trips to Shiloh, her religious nature, and her tender heart that she must have asked God about her barrenness many times. But that's part of the mystery of prayer. There was something about the faith and desperation in her prayer *that day* at the Tabernacle. God was the only one who could help her, and she knew it.

Hannah broke through whatever the barrier was when she completely surrendered to God and believed him to do the impossible. We must pray with that same spirit, "God, it is hopeless, and we are helpless to change anything. You *must* intervene in our lives and churches. We *must* bear fruit, but we can't without your blessing."

## LESSONS FROM HANNAH

All changes — spiritual revivals, a turnaround in a church, a barren life now bearing fruit — begin when there is a discontentment that says, "I refuse to accept this."

As this storm of spiritual decline and absence of personal transformation hits the church, we can't accept the damage being done. If we rationalize and make excuses for why things are the way they are, if we blame secular humanism or immoral laws and bad government, we will never follow Hannah's path and witness God changing our situation.

God loves us, and he takes no joy in our spiritual decline. We *must* settle that fact in our minds. He is not rejoicing that ministers are leaving the ministry in record numbers, or that the gospel is not being spread effectively. God takes no delight in, nor did he ordain, that churches decline and Christians live without his blessing. God does not rejoice in any of that. What parent would take joy in seeing their child struggle and be defeated? If we are hungry for something more, will God not satisfy us? If he gave us his Son, will he not also now give us all that we need to live for him on earth?

He has chosen us as the ones through whom he will work on planet Earth. He is not in partnership with the Republicans or the Democrats. It's the church of Jesus Christ or nothing. We are his body. Although he is the head, the head cannot properly function without the cooperation of a healthy body. The mind of Christ has the answers we need, but the body has to be healthy enough to carry out those orders.

God is waiting for us to rise up with faith in his promises. He wants us to return to *his* plan for *his* church. Then we will see things happen that we couldn't even imagine! God wants to turn things around. But as in the days of Hannah, he is waiting for someone to say, "No more; I refuse to accept this!" We can't sugarcoat it, live in denial, or accept it as the new normal.

Those Christians who emphasize the sovereignty of God — almost to the exclusion of his love — usually reject any teaching about God's people being stirred to seek him in a fresh way. They feel God is somehow just fine with the sad condition of his church or he would change it, wouldn't he? Oddly, I have noticed that these same Christians move heaven and earth to help their kids when they are hurting and cry out for help. Do we love *our* children more than God loves his? Many believe God is going to do what he wants when he wants, so why bother asking him in faith for anything? But Hannah's prayer proves otherwise. God hears our cries and answers. In the midst of the storm he is there to help us if we accept our powerlessness and cry out for his power to save us.

## A GENERATION DEFINED BY PRAYERLESSNESS

Unfortunately, because of the growing tide within certain circles against anything supernatural, there is less emphasis on prayer than ever before. Could it be there is even an unspoken denial that God answers prayer? What else would explain our lack of emphasis on prayer?

Consider these three examples:

Example 1: A few years ago, a couple of pastors on my staff attended a church growth conference held in another city. The hook was that the presiding church growth expert would provide the perfect formula that pastors needed. It was all about the "cutting-edge" technology (lights, sound, multimedia) and clever new ideas that would turn the tide. The pastors later told me they had heard some good ideas, mostly on style and methodology, but heard little reference made to biblical truth. It was more like an Apple convention than a Bible-centered, prayerful time of spiritual refreshing.

But what struck them was that during the two-and-a-half days there was not one minute of corporate prayer. Of course, there was the perfunctory prayer by someone at the beginning of the main sessions, but not even five minutes given to corporate prayer, where these pastors could wait before God. No time was allotted for them to pray for each other and imitate the apostolic church: "They devoted themselves to the apostles' teaching and to the fellowship, to the breaking of bread and *to prayer*" (Acts 2:42).

Think about how we pastors need such times at the throne of grace to receive fresh wisdom and strength from God to combat all the assaults of the enemy. How could a Christian conference of *any* kind not focus on the Word and prayer? This kind of leadership model will in the end have a chilling effect on the spiritual life of any church. It is behind much of our decline even as it promises growth and success.

Example 2: Recently a pastor of another congregation in the South stopped by to ask for advice. He was trying to find ways to incorporate more prayer into his church, but it wasn't working.

"What should I do?" he asked me. "When I tried to lead into times of prayer during Sunday services, the people got fidgety."

Essentially, the unspoken message from the congregation was: "Say something. Do something. Or sing something. But don't just stand there and tell us to talk to God." This pastor had obviously not made clear to his congregation that God's house is still to be called a house of prayer.

Example 3: I could cite countless examples of conversations, emails, and letters from people who love Jesus, love their Bibles, and are hungry to find a church where they can grow. They're looking for their churches to be houses of prayer and frustrated that prayer isn't a priority in their local congregation.

One especially poignant letter came from the wife of a church deacon. She had read something about the power of prayer in one of my books, and God used it to provoke her to study the prayers found in the Bible. She was both convicted and inspired. She also knew her church seemed to be struggling and lethargic. She made an appointment to see her pastor and with a sincere spirit said, "Pastor, the church is struggling a bit; we're not growing, and converts aren't being made. I was wondering if maybe we should consider a new emphasis on prayer? Since there's very little prayer in our church, perhaps we should consider starting a prayer meeting, or maybe you could teach a series on prayer."

The pastor interrupted and said, "That's not the style of church we have. We have a different model. We're not into prayer."

She was dumbstruck.

The obvious question she shared with me was, how could you be a Christian church and ignore all of the Bible passages about the power and importance of prayer? If God honors and answers prayer, to "not be into prayer" is the same as not being into God. If the Lord is alive, wouldn't the church want to talk with him?

These aren't isolated examples. This is happening all over America, and it is the lament of spiritually minded people who sense that something is amiss. This is especially sad to see in churches where the pastor is famous as a great expositor and teacher. Whatever his content and gifting might be, it's strange that the bottom line result is basically a prayerless church. Discerning believers feel the lack of the Spirit's power and the absence of a holy excitement about the risen Christ. This lady's concern and spiritual dissatisfaction are not unusual. They are being felt everywhere.

> **If God honors and answers prayer, to "not be into prayer" is the same as not being into God.**

How odd is this when the Bible is so clear about the importance of prayer? It is written in Isaiah, "My house will be called a house of prayer" (56:7). In Jeremiah, God says, "Call to me and I will answer you" (33:3). Jesus says, "Ask and it will be given to you; seek and you will find; knock and the door will be opened to you" (Matt. 7:7). And James writes, "You do not have because you do not ask God" (James 4:2).

Whether we are Calvinist or Arminian, evangelical or charismatic, how can we really believe in the Bible — God's Holy Word — while our churches are failing to be houses of prayer? Today in the contemporary church, there seems to be a practical denial of the efficacy of prayer. We treasure teaching, we enjoy praise and worship, and some of us look forward to times of fellowship with other believers. All of these are important and have their place in God's purposes for us. But it is vital to remember what most have forgotten: God's house is to be called, not a house of teaching, or of worship, or of fellowship, but a house of prayer!

Sadly, not only can many churches not be called a house of prayer, but also there is hardly *any element* of prayer within. This in turn has also contributed to a prayerlessness in the individual lives of Christians. If the pastoral leadership doesn't value prayer, how important could it really be? I don't want to be critical of my peers, but with all of these biblical promises and commands, how can there still be so many prayerless people and churches?

I have come to the sad conclusion that Christians have lost faith in God's promises concerning prayer. How else can we explain why prayer isn't paramount in our lives and in our churches? If we believed his promises, wouldn't we sometimes preach entire series about prayer? Wouldn't we make room for prayer in Sunday services and set aside weekly times where we could together learn to call on God for his help? We would — unless we are convinced that the status quo is acceptable and we don't need help from heaven.

The key to prayer that changes things is a deep sense of inadequacy and helplessness among God's people. This is why Jesus himself arose early to talk with his Father in a place isolated from others. He felt he couldn't face the day without the Father's help and direction. When Christian churches and individual believers feel smugly self-sufficient, the Spirit of prayer becomes stifled. Even a growing knowledge of Bible truth can puff us up to the point where we lose that childlike dependence on the Lord for daily help.

This subtle denial of the power and value of prayer is also a denial of God's love for us. If God already gave us his Son to die on the cross, would he not also, in love, give us everything else we need to live the Christian life and spread the gospel message? Our challenge is not to try to figure out a detailed theology of prayer. Our challenge is just to obey the Bible and have faith that when we pray, God will answer. *Lord, teach us to pray.*

## TOO BUSY NOT TO PRAY

The great devotional writer Andrew Bonar laments in his spiritual *Diary* that he was so busy in the ministry, running and taking care of things, that he became deeply convicted that his days were filled with much activity, but little prayer. Then he realized that prayer wasn't for the purpose of helping the work, but that prayer *was* the work. From the main work of prayer, fruitful ministry and fruitful living will result, because prayer secures the help of God. If we are really looking for formulas that will strengthen our lives and grow our churches, let's all begin by coming to God with our needs (Heb. 4:16).

Martin Luther said, "Whoever prays well, studies well," because he knew that drawing near to God would facilitate Bible study and the understanding of the Word of God. If the leadership of our churches and Christians in the pew would start going to God in Hannah-like prayer, just think of the dynamic changes God would make in our pastoral ministries and church services!

When we bring our problems and burdens to God in prayer, he has promised that the Holy Spirit would help us pray with power (Rom. 8:26). That kind of prayer becomes irresistible before God, because he's the one who's inspiring it! Why else would he help us pray through the Holy Spirit if he weren't going to do something about it? Possibly the least understood privilege given to us as Christians is "praying in the Spirit" (Jude 20; Eph. 6:18).

Hannah did more than pray. She *poured out her soul* to God, and we need to do the same. The only way to learn how to pray like that is by doing it. Symposiums, books (including this one), and conferences on prayer can all be helpful, but the deepest secrets of prayer are only learned by spending time with God.

Imagine if churches would just stop everything, for one day a week (or even one day a month), so time could be set aside for prayer. None of us can even imagine the awesome answers God would send in response to our turning back to him.

How can unbelievers be reached effectively if we Christians don't change first? "If my people, who are called by my name, will humble themselves and pray and seek my face and turn from their wicked ways, then will I hear from heaven, and I will forgive their sin and will heal their land" (2 Chron. 7:14). This famous passage was not meant for atheists or agnostics, but for God's own people.

If we look at society today, if we look at the challenge of a country becoming more godless by the week, if we look at laws being passed that mock any form of morality—instead of lamenting and protesting, wouldn't it be better for us to plead with God to visit his people? We need to move toward God, and it begins with desperate prayer. "But it's not practical," someone might say. "You gotta get involved in the process." But that *is* God's process exactly! Where has political activism with an increasing exclusion of prayer over the last twenty-five years brought us? Have we seen America move toward God? Have we seen the Christian church draw closer to God? Only a different approach can bring different results.

But what would happen if we started opening the doors of our churches for a prayer meeting?

"Our church isn't like that," you might say. "No one would show up."

Maybe not. But maybe *one* would.

Maybe it would be someone like the woman who, in the midst of her own personal storm, knelt at our noon prayer meeting, pouring out her heart to God about her son.

**The goal for all churches and Christians today is simple: We must bear fruit. Jesus clearly taught this.**

Maybe the one would be like Hannah, and God would use her desperate prayer to affect a church and circle of friends that could then eventually change a town or city.

Hannah reminds us that although we have stumbled, and none of us are what we should be, God can arm us with his strength. And if we are hungry, dissatisfied, and frustrated, he can provide fulfillment.

"Elkanah made love to his wife Hannah, and *the LORD remembered her*" (1 Sam. 1:19).

How did the baby come about? Because the Lord remembered Hannah.

What about Hannah did he remember? He remembered Hannah's desperate prayer.

He couldn't forget that prayer; more importantly, he couldn't deny that prayer. Some may think that might sound like a presumptuous way to describe a sovereign God, but that is what the Bible tells us. He remembered Hannah, and she conceived and gave birth to a son — Samuel. God used her craving to bear fruit and her anguished desire for a child to lead her to change the history of Israel.

The goal for all churches and Christians today is simple: We must bear fruit. Jesus clearly taught this: "This is to my Father's glory, that you bear much fruit, showing yourselves to be my disciples.... (I) appointed you so that you might *go* and bear fruit" (John 15:8, 16). Unfortunately, the truth is that most of our churches and believers are not bearing much fruit.

Like Hannah, we can love God, but be barren. But we don't have to accept it.

We can go to God in our desperate Hannah-like prayer and ask him to make us fruitful. When God answers our prayers, it humbles us, and we can't praise him enough the way Hannah did (1 Sam. 2:1 – 10). After all, what could Hannah boast in? That she got desperate and wept quietly before God? Hannah was humbled for the rest of her life, especially when people congratulated her on having a boy like Samuel. Deep down she knew how it all happened. It was in her son Samuel's name.

She had been heard by God.

# Chapter 4

# SHELTER FROM THE STORM

Avril's Story

*Consider a prisoner just released from prison, an immigrant trying to create a new life in a foreign country, or a pregnant woman who just left an abusive relationship. How would they go about furnishing their first apartment? Chances are, they are already living below the poverty line, barely making enough for rent and other necessities such as food and clothing. A new sofa or kitchen table is a luxury they can't afford.*

*At our church, God has raised up a unique ministry that provides furniture and small appliances to people who need them. If a member is getting rid of used items in good working condition, the Acts Ministry will send a representative to their house to collect them. They then warehouse the items until they identify someone who needs them.*

*What's really special about this ministry is that it was founded by the unlikeliest person you could imagine — a former homeless woman. Avril DeJesus will tell you she didn't think she was supposed to lead the Acts Ministry, but after her own Hannah-like prayer, God showed her she was his choice. Since then, she has led this growing ministry with love and compassion, demonstrating how God can use a faithful believer to provide shelter from the storms of life.*

*I'll let her tell you how it happened in her own words.*

## AVRIL

Miranda was only three months old the day I found her lying in her crib and not breathing. The EMTs did their best to revive Miranda while on the way to the hospital, but it was too late. Despite the horror of the situation, I remained in control at the hospital and dutifully signed all the papers. When I returned home to my other two children without her, I didn't break down. I didn't scream or cry. In fact, I didn't even shed a tear that entire day.

Growing up, I had gone to church with my godmother. I don't remember anyone telling me as a child that I needed to be saved and to give my life to Christ. But even without knowing that, somehow I believed God was real and I knew my life wasn't right. I also feared for my baby's soul. I didn't know if my choices would affect where her soul would spend eternity.

That night, all alone, I knelt down beside my bed and prayed. "God, I know I haven't been a good person. I know I'm living in sin because I'm not married to my children's father. But if you will take Miranda into heaven, and if you will not hold my sins against her, I promise I will take the other children to church. I will make sure they grow up going to church and knowing who you are."

Before I even spoke the last word, I felt I heard a voice. It wasn't audible as if it was in the room; it was as if I heard it echoing throughout my body. It seemed to say, "She's already here."

That's the moment I broke down and cried. I'm sure some of it was grief and sorrow, but most of all it felt like relief. I felt such joy after that answer to prayer!

Even though I knew Miranda was already in heaven, I kept my part of the bargain. I took my kids to church that Sunday, and I have been taking them to church ever since. And not long after Miranda's death, I married their father, and God blessed us with a little girl we called Christina.

A few years later, on a June morning in 1986, I stood at the sink washing dishes when I heard a "thump-thump-thump" at my door. It wasn't an ordinary knock; it was the sound of a massive fist pounding the worn, wooden door. My heart skipped a beat.

"Who's there?" I asked.

"US marshals," a deep voice said. "Open up!"

I quickly wiped off my soapy hands, and I glanced at my kids. My five-year-old daughter, Shannon, was playing with her dolls on the floor, and Christina, my two-year-old, was still strapped in the high chair. Fortunately, Adrian, my oldest, was at school finishing up the last few days in third grade before summer break.

As I moved toward the door, I scanned my furnished apartment and mentally made a checklist of things I might need to gather: diapers, bottles, toys, coats and shoes, important papers, and medicines. *And snacks, I can't forget snacks for the kids.* I knew that once the door opened, I had maybe fifteen minutes before I would have to walk out with the girls and leave the rest of my possessions behind. I let out a deep sigh and reached for the knob.

"What's going on?" I asked.

They carried guns; I'd forgotten that.

"Your rent hasn't been paid," the tallest marshal said, flashing his badge.

I could see the landlord standing behind him.

"Hold on a minute, let me make a call," I said as much to convince myself as them that it was all a mistake that easily could be fixed with a phone call. This wasn't the first time the marshals had come, yet I had always been able to find someone to loan us money to pay our rent.

But this time, the landlord refused.

The taller marshal stepped inside and looked at the children and then at me. "I'll give you twenty minutes to get yourself together," he said.

I quickly grabbed a plastic bag and began to fill it.

Most people know when they will be evicted. They have already received multiple overdue notices and citations from the landlord. I'm sure that happened in our case too, but I wasn't aware of it. Our marriage was strained, and my husband controlled the finances. I never knew when the electricity was about to be turned off, or when we would be without water for a week. And during our short marriage, we had moved at least ten times.

I swiftly but carefully chose a change of clothes for each of us. I knew it was unlikely we would ever see any of our belongings again. As I packed up a few of our personal items, my only concern was for the children. I wanted to keep calm so they wouldn't be upset. I didn't cry or get angry. I grew up in a very strict home, and I was not allowed to show emotions. Being proper and having good manners was encouraged. Feelings were not. I had learned early on to master my emotions and to do what I could to keep from upsetting others.

"Shannon, pick out your favorite doll and bring it to me so I can pack it," I said.

"Why?"

I paused. What could I tell her? I couldn't tell her the truth, that we were being kicked out onto the street.

"Because we're going to the park, and I want you to take it with you," I said.

Shannon chose the baby doll and handed it to me.

> I grew up in a very strict home, and I was not allowed to show emotions Being proper and having good manners was encouraged. Feelings were not.
> —*Avril*

After I had gathered what I could reasonably carry, I picked up Christina, balanced her on my left hip, and grabbed Shannon's pudgy fingers in my right hand. The three plastic grocery bags on my arm now held everything we owned.

"Let's go," I said, leading the way out.

I heard the marshals padlock the front door, but I refused to look back. I was humiliated that this had happened again. I knew my neighbors were watching, and I couldn't bear the thought of them talking behind my back.

I was officially homeless.

Adrian would get out of school in a few hours, so the only thing I could do was wait. The kids and I headed to the park across the street. *But then what?*

While I was at the park with the smaller children, waiting for Adrian to get out of school, we called friends who were on their way out of town. They let us stay in their apartment for three weeks while they were away.

When those weeks were up, my husband came up with a plan to send the children and me to his mother in Georgia, since his aunt in the Bronx only had room for him. I didn't want to go, although I didn't know where to go. When we missed the train, I called a friend I had met just recently. She said that we could stay with her family.

During the next fifteen months, we moved five more times. Generous friends allowed us to stay, moving their kids out of their bedrooms so my family could use them. We slept on sofas and floors, in a studio, and in a one-bedroom apartment. The largest place we stayed was a two-bedroom apartment with a friend who also had three children.

In February, at seven months pregnant and eight months after we were evicted, I moved into a shelter. My husband and I had been living apart for most of that time, and our marriage was further strained. I sensed it would end in divorce. I knew that one day I would be the sole provider for my kids. I needed to build a life that could support us.

It was a relief to have a place we could call home, even if it was a shelter. I had managed to keep Adrian in the same school despite our moves. Fortunately, the shelter was blocks from Adrian's school, and they would let us stay there for up to a year. And without the stress of living with other families or the pressure of figuring out where we could live next, I finally had the freedom to think about our future.

All that time in church with my kids had paid off. I had become a believer in Jesus Christ, and I knew that whatever happened, God was in control. He would take care of us; he had already proven that the night Miranda died.

Strange as it may sound, staying at the shelter was a wonderful experience. For the first time in months, I didn't have to worry about where we were going to live or feel uncomfortable because I was inconveniencing someone else.

While at the shelter, I gave birth to my fourth child, a son I named "Richie." Because I had not been living with my husband and I only saw him occasionally, I felt as if I was a widow and my kids were orphans. Knowing a divorce was on the horizon and fearful of the future for my beautiful children and myself, I began to examine how I had gotten myself into this mess. Ashamed of my situation, I looked to my Lord Jesus, whom I had recently come to know as my Savior. Sunday services at church were my source of nourishment. I learned so much from the sermons and drank in the Spirit, letting him flood me with love and hope. For the first time, I allowed my tears to flow freely as I daily consecrated my life and my children to the Lord.

One Sunday, Pastor Cymbala preached a sermon I will never forget. He called it "God's Other Chosen People: Orphans, Widows, and Foreigners." It focused on God's concern for the most weak, vulnerable people within the nation of Israel. God gave various commands to help provide for them and warned his own people to be sure not to take advantage of them. It made me realize that as a single parent, I had a special privilege. When I called on the Lord, he would hear me. In the eyes of man, I was still a "welfare mother" — a term I detested — but in God's eyes, I was his child. In addition, my difficult plight in life made him sensitive to my prayers. It was a promise he would keep over and over again.

We lived in the shelter for almost a year, during which time the kids and I thrived. But then we had to move.

Through a series of circumstances, we ended up in an apartment in the South Bronx, an area called Fort Apache, one of the most poor and dangerous areas in the city. Though the apartment was clean, it was infested with large rats, and I worried about Richie, who was only seven months old.

I had no furniture. When you get evicted, all of your stuff goes into storage, and you have to pay to get it out. If you can't afford to pay the storage fees, they sell it to pay off your debt.

Fortunately, one of the pastors at Brooklyn Tabernacle became aware of my situation. Pastor Hannon was like a father figure to me. He had planned to give his son some furniture he no longer used, but he realized my need and one day showed up at my apartment and began unloading it from his car. He carried it in and placed every piece where I directed. I was so thankful for his thoughtfulness and generosity. The furniture was more than a practical gift; it was also an emotional one. It showed me that someone cared, and it made my house feel like a home.

Church members offered me small appliances, or clothes and toys for the kids. I was grateful for whatever they gave me. What I couldn't use I gave away to someone who could.

I lived in that apartment for a year and a half before moving to an apartment in Brooklyn. Eventually, the woman who ran the shelter I once lived in opened a second one and asked me to be the house mom. Living and working there, I was able to go back to college and get my degree. After graduating, I moved out and had to furnish an apartment all over again.

Each time I moved, people would hear about our needs, and they would give us a bag with stuff in it. Those bags always excited me.

Every item of clothing that the children and I had came from one of these bags. People donated furniture and small appliances. Soon I had more than I needed, and out of my abundance, I wanted to find a way to give back.

One Sunday, I invited some friends to what I called a "blessing fellowship." It was an informal get-together. We would meet at my house for dinner after church, but after we

**Soon I had more than I needed, and out of my abundance, I wanted to find a way to give back.**

*—Avril*

ate I would take them into a room where I had laid out all the things I'd been given but couldn't use. I would make it look like a boutique, and then I would tell my guests they could go "shopping" and take whatever they wanted. While the women picked through the clothes looking for just the right size, the kids squealed in delight examining the toys and choosing the ones they wanted.

The women were so excited and thankful that I started doing the blessing fellowships more frequently. As people heard about them, they would give me more bags saying, "I know you'll find someone who can use this."

But soon, the amount of stuff I had been given started accumulating faster than I could give it away. Around this time, I was hired to work at the church. We had a very large adult learning center, with hundreds of students all working toward their GEDs. Obviously, these men and women didn't have the education that they needed, and some couldn't even read or write. Others were new to the country and couldn't speak English. These people were the poorest of the poor.

So I started bringing in toasters or blenders, small pieces of furniture, and clean clothes for them to wear on job interviews.

"Can anybody use this?" I'd ask, and they were always delighted to accept it. Often they were so thankful that they would tell someone else, who would then come to me and say, "I wear a size ten; do you have any more dresses?" Or "Do you have an extra toaster?"

Over the years, God even blessed me with donated cars that helped me deliver the furniture. There were a couple of young people who helped me deliver, and we would borrow or rent a truck if something larger was needed. I started letting the pastors at Brooklyn Tabernacle know what I was doing, and they started bringing me people they were ministering to who had needs. Soon the pastors were donating furniture too.

Pastor Alex Burgos had great taste in furniture, and one day he called and invited me to his house. There he showed us an amazing living room set. "You think somebody can use this?" he asked.

A few days later we were able to use his furniture to bless a young couple who had just gotten married and moved into their first apartment.

Everything continued to grow. I found unused storage space at the church and claimed it as a place to temporarily hold the things I was accumulating. The church also allowed me to use its vans when making especially large deliveries.

One day a sister from church called and said, "I have a freezer I'm getting rid of. It's in really great condition. Can I donate that?"

"Let me get back to you," I said. No one had ever asked us for a freezer, and we really didn't have a place to store it. I needed time to think about it.

Just two days later, a young mom with a bunch of kids called and wanted to know if I had a freezer! "It would really help us keep our food costs down if we could buy it in bulk and freeze it," she said.

So no one had ever asked for a freezer, but as soon as one was offered, it was matched with a need. This kind of thing happened frequently. God was faithful.

The needs kept increasing, but the donations always seemed to keep pace. Someone would request a very specific piece of furniture. "I need a small table, and it has to be rectangular to fit in my kitchen because my apartment is so tiny," came one request.

Later that day, someone called to find out how to donate a table with those exact specifications. I saw God's provision over and over again.

It was as if God multiplied everything and I couldn't get rid of the stuff fast enough. The more I gave away, the more people gave me. I couldn't outgive God. Soon the bags were overtaking our living areas, and the kids were begging me to get them out of the house.

Eventually, the amount of stuff I was accumulating was bigger than my home and car could hold. I approached the church about starting a ministry and spoke with a pastor and told him how great the need was. I explained my background and my passion for helping *the least of these* to have clothes and furnishings as tangible proof of God's love for them.

"Okay, how are you going to do it?" he asked.

"Oh, I'm not going to do it," I said.

"If you want a ministry, you're going to have to start it yourself," he said.

I didn't think I was the right person to take on the ministry, but I promised I would pray about finding someone.

A good friend from church, who saw how much we were growing, offered to join me in prayer for the ministry. I would stop by her house on the way home from work on Wednesdays, and we would pray expectantly for more storage space and additional help.

I had been using the church vans for about six months when I got some really bad news. The church was going to sell the vans to raise funds for some expansion we were doing to the building. I was crushed! My car was no longer big enough to make the pickups and deliveries, and I was desperate to help these people. I didn't know what to do. So I prayed.

"Lord, what am I going to do if they sell the vans? My car is not big enough for this ministry. What should I do?"

I felt like the Lord said to me, "Buy the van."

But I thought that inner voice couldn't be God. Every car I had ever owned had been donated to me. So I continued to pray, waiting on the Lord's answer. Once again, I felt as though the Lord said to me, "*You* buy the van."

Because my husband and I had divorced, it was necessary for me to tightly control our spending. I had always been very frugal, and I had savings in the bank. Although purchasing a car didn't feel right to me, I didn't trust my feelings; instead, I trusted God. I paid cash for the van and used it to expand our services.

My heart was enlarged by the love I had for those who needed our services most. Each time I made a delivery, I was able to encourage the people with whom I met. "I've been where you are," I would tell them. "I was once homeless too, but I put my trust in Jesus." I could see that the hope meant just as much to them — maybe more — as the furniture did.

As my burden grew, and the organization increased in size and complexity, so did the leadership vacuum. There was no one to run it. On my own, I tried several things, and at one point I even rented a storefront. I thought those with needs could "shop" for what they needed, but the storefront didn't work out. Something needed to change, but I didn't know what.

One day when I'd had enough, I threw myself on the floor of my bedroom and cried until the carpet was wet. I prayed to God, begging him for help.

> I felt a bit the way Peter must have felt stepping out of the boat and onto the water. I had to trust that if God said do it, he would give me whatever I needed to get it done.
>
> —*Avril*

"God, why would you give me this burden, and then not give me a way to do it? I have this burning in my soul to help people get what they need, so they can know you care about all their needs. But we need a leader to take this to the next level, so we can help more people in your name."

At times I pounded my fists on the floor. "God, what are you going to do? How are you going to do this?"

When the tears slowed and I calmed down a bit, I once again heard God speak to me.

"Go ahead and do it," he said.

"What do you mean, go ahead and do it? How? How do I do it? What do I do?"

"*You* do it."

"But how? What do I do? How do I do it?"

"Do it."

Though I continued to pray, I didn't hear anything else but "Do it."

When I stopped praying, I was sure God wanted me to lead the ministry. I had no idea what the next step was, but as I stood up, I knew I had to put one foot in front of the other until I figured it out. I felt a bit the way Peter must have felt stepping out of the boat and onto the water. I had to trust that if God said do it, he would give me whatever I needed to get it done.

That was the turning point. From then on, I prayed for each resource as I needed it. For example, one day I said, "God, I really need more help. I need you to send helpers."

And he sent me people. Amazing people! Lawyers and accountants, people who loved God, and people who cared about others. They joined me in prayer and in service.

One of the people God sent was a staff member of the church. He began helping to pick up and deliver furniture, and before long we were dating. That man is now my husband.

We stopped doing the clothing giveaways, so we could concentrate on furniture — something no one else was doing. We became an official ministry of the church. We leased a warehouse for storing donations until they were needed. The Acts Ministry is so large now that we do furniture distribution every Saturday, sometimes making several stops for pickups and deliveries.

It has been a blessing to me to see people in need receive the furnishings that make a house a home. But it is an equal blessing to see the joy of the people who donate the furniture, knowing that their possessions will go to someone in need. When we make a pickup or delivery, our team prays for each person and family and always tries to bless their homes.

On Saturdays, teams gather together for "mission reports," where they jubilantly share the stories of the people they met that week. Recently one team member reported taking furniture to a single parent — a Muslim woman. He asked if he could pray with her, knowing that the religious differences might make her want to decline the offer. However, she said yes. As he prayed with her, she wept. Afterward, she told him how thankful she was, not only for the furniture, but also for the prayer.

Moments like that make the challenges and hardships my kids and I faced so much more meaningful. I understand these people; I know what they're feeling because I've been there. Being able to give a bit of my time and energy to help those in similar situations is an incredible blessing. I am so thankful for the amazing life I am able to lead. I pray every day that my abundance can bless those in need with the knowledge that God loves them and cares about *all* of their needs.

Recently I shared in our church a bit of information about the ministry. I told them how God heard my desperate prayer and his unexpected answer to me was simply, "Do it." So out of obedience to him and love for those in need, I did it. After I finished speaking, Pastor Cymbala told the congregation, "God can turn your mess into your ministry."

He certainly did mine.

# Chapter 5

# A LIGHT IN THE STORM

Leaders Who Love God and His People

The religious atmosphere in Hannah's time was truly tragic. The people of Israel were doing what was right in their own eyes, with little thought of God. At the root of the problem was the nation's spiritual leadership. The people were a reflection of those in charge in Shiloh, the center of religious worship at the time.

Eli was the high priest at the house of the Lord in Shiloh. He and his sons were the divinely appointed leaders of Israel. They were from the priestly line of Aaron and were part of the covenant people of God, offering sacrifices for the people according to the law of Moses.

However, Eli was spiritually half-asleep and lacking discernment. When Hannah was praying her desperate prayer, Eli had no clue that she was crying out to God.

> Hannah was praying in her heart, and her lips were moving but her voice was not heard. Eli … said to her, "How long are you going to stay drunk? Put away your wine."
>
> "Not so, my lord," Hannah replied, "I am a woman who is deeply troubled. I have not been drinking wine or beer; I was pouring out my soul to the LORD" (1 Sam. 1:13–15).

Hannah, a simple woman with no appointed spiritual position, was more spiritually in tune with God than the ordained leadership of the nation. Eli, the high priest, was so out of touch that he couldn't discern that the humble woman before him was praying one of the greatest prayers of the Old Testament. He thought she was drunk!

Even worse, Eli's sons were ready to succeed their father as priests. The Bible says of them, "Eli's sons were scoundrels; they had no regard for the LORD" (1 Sam. 2:12). So we have a half-blind, spiritually insensitive high priest, whose sons were abusing their authority and taking advantage of the people. They regularly took for themselves the offerings that were brought to Shiloh for God. The Bible says that this sin was "very great in the LORD's sight, for they were treating the LORD's offering with contempt" (v. 17).

I am sure that the sons had excuses for their selfishness and that many of the people respected their priestly positions. But the quality of spiritual leadership can only be measured by how it looks *in the Lord's sight*.

Eventually every believer, including pastors, will stand at the judgment seat of Christ (Rom. 14:10; 2 Cor. 5:10). On that day we will have brought before us the quality of our lives and labor for Christ. What others think about us will be totally irrelevant. Our excuses and self-justification will also cease as we appear before Christ. For those of us who are ministers, the judgment will be even stricter. "Not many of you should become teachers, my fellow believers, because you know that we who teach will be judged more strictly" (James 3:1).

What is wholesome spiritual leadership in the Lord's sight will always lead to greater spiritual health among God's people. This is very precious work in the Lord's eyes. Everything else, no matter how temporarily popular, will prove to be wood, hay, and stubble in the end. That's why we must pray that God will raise up godly, sacrificial leaders to build Christ's church and act as a light in the gathering gloom of the storm.

## THE LEADERSHIP STATUS QUO ISN'T WORKING

Look, I have written a bunch of books, but this is the hardest chapter I've *ever* tried to write because in it I want to talk honestly about myself and my fellow leaders. I don't want to be hypercritical, yet at the same time some difficult things need to be said. I am dissatisfied with myself not only with so much that I preached in the past, but also when I'm not operating with the fullest blessing of God on my current efforts. When I consider how the Lord has used men and women in the past to make a deep spiritual impact on the world around them, I grow discontented and want more grace from God.

It is to be hoped that we are all sincere people who have been called by God into the ministry and into positions of service. I also include Christians who don't hold an official title but wield spiritual influence in their families, workplaces, and communities. Here is what is evident:

> Most leadership models we have today are often faulty and unbiblical.
> The Christian church in general is growing lukewarm.
> As a result, Christianity in America is in a nosedive.
> All the data confirm these unfortunate truths.

Again, I don't want to come across as hypercritical. I am too frail and faulty myself to act as judge, but our problems do need an open and honest analysis. We all need to step up and serve Jesus better if we care about his kingdom expanding. I know better than anyone else how often I've failed!

In an effort to begin the conversation, though, I would like to compare our approach versus how Jesus ministered and how the apostles later built the Christian church. Then we should ask, "What does the Lord think about our efforts?"

> **We all need to step up and serve Jesus better if we care about his kingdom expanding. I know better than anyone else how often I've failed!**

## We Lead with Dry Business Principles

The growing emphasis among Christian leaders over the last twenty years or so has been to make a drastic move away from the models of Paul, Peter, and the other apostles found in the New Testament. While much is different culturally for us in the twenty-first century, we have almost totally lost God's New Testament directives for competent spiritual ministry. Often replacing those godly role models has been the highly organized business leader who "gets things done" and knows what "works" in the marketplace. This "pastor as CEO" theme is prevalent in many popular leadership conferences that America's pastors attend.

### But Paul Led with Tears

It is clear that the apostle Paul never attempted to be the successful business-leader type so many pastors aspire to be. In Acts 20, Paul gives his farewell address to the Ephesian church leaders. In it, he warns them to be careful in their duties and reminds them what his leadership looked like: "Remember that for three years I never stopped warning each of you night and day with tears" (Acts 20:31).

Paul's leadership involved such passionate concern that it produced tears!

But he also saw incredible results from his heartfelt efforts. Paul didn't need a business model for growing the Christian church; he simply followed Jesus' command in spreading the gospel, he depended on the Holy Spirit, and he added lots of prayer and tears of love. He became a tender servant of not only Christ, but also the believers.

### We Attract Followers

Compare Paul's mind-set with the obvious ego problems prevalent in much of our ministry today. Vast audiences hanging on every word spoken can become a dangerous drug. Some larger-than-life personalities have their own groupies who think everything they do is great and that everything they say is true even when it is not backed up by the Bible. It becomes more about what *they* teach than what Almighty God says in his Word.

The Lord often uses his servants in incredible ways, and we are all thankful to God for that. But we have too many believers today who aren't into *Christ* as much as some famous teacher's ministry, another pastor's television show, or the newest formula for doing church. It's sad to sit at lunch with six or seven pastors and rarely hear mention of the living Christ and Bible truth, but tons about some teacher's style and creative ideas. Paul sets us straight on this point: "So neither the one who plants nor the one who waters is *anything,* but only God, who makes things grow" (1 Cor. 3:7). No one is anyone — it should all be about God.

### But Paul Attracts Followers to Jesus

Even in the early church, Paul saw teachers who were full of themselves, attracting disciples rather than pointing them to Jesus. "Even from your own number men will arise and distort the truth in order to *draw away disciples after them*" (Acts 20:30). Not after another god, mind you, but after *themselves*. Paul admonished the members of the church at Corinth for saying, "'I follow Paul'; another, 'I follow Apollos'; another, 'I follow Cephas'" (1 Cor. 1:12). Paul warns that these little fan clubs only cause division within the one body of Christ and are a sign of carnality.

This is what happens when some ministers subtly draw attention to their particular ministry as being a little more special than anyone else's. We should always be on guard against those self-important leaders who represent the opposite spirit of the meek and lowly Jesus.

## We Preach Entertaining Messages

Worse than that, there is also a growing trend to water down the true gospel of Christ. The thought is that it's better if folks leave "feeling good about themselves" rather than convicted of sin and needing the Savior. Some leaders feel that candid talk about sex or that using profanity will be the "hook" rather than the simple gospel preaching God has blessed for centuries. Others sound more like stand-up comics whose goal is to provide mostly humor.

I receive hundreds of emails from individuals who ask me if I know of a church near them that still preaches the simple, pure Word of God. They complain that their pastor rarely references the Bible. Others write asking me to recommend a church with a prayer meeting. They say very little if any time is dedicated for prayer in their churches.

What if, instead of using our own cleverness and intelligence, leaders relied on the truth found in God's Word delivered in love through the power of the Holy Spirit? God would certainly be more pleased, and the Bible assures us that the spiritual results would be amazing. Guaranteed!

## But the Disciples Preach the Gospel

Sure, entertaining talks can draw crowds, but so do Broadway shows. When Peter first preached the gospel of Jesus, the audience was "cut to the heart" (Acts 2:37), rather than being amused or impressed by the presentation. Not only were three thousand people baptized, but their lives were also transformed by Christ.

As a result of their conversion,

> They devoted themselves to the apostles' teaching and to fellowship, to the breaking of bread and to prayer.... All the believers were together and had everything in common. They sold

property and possessions to give to anyone who had need. Every day they continued to meet together in the temple courts. They broke bread in their homes and ate together with glad and sincere hearts, praising God and enjoying the favor of all the people (Acts 2:42, 44 – 47a).

Does that picture even faintly resemble the results we see in our churches? Yet that's why God inspired Luke to describe what the early Christian church looked like. He wants us to make that our model.

**God inspired Luke to describe what the early Christian church looked like. He wants us to make that our model.**

Not only were these folks born-again believers in Jesus, but they also began sharing the gospel with others effectively. "And the Lord added to their number daily those who were being saved" (Acts 2:47b). If we aren't giving believers nourishment today in the form of good spiritual food, how can they grow and be healthy? How will they reproduce themselves in seeing others accept Christ? The people who come to our churches are facing spiritual battles we can't imagine, and we're tossing them M&Ms! This is why so many, instead of becoming mature and ministering to others, stay chronically weak and bear little fruit.

### We Become Discouraged

I want to cry when I see the statistics on how many pastors leave the ministry each month. I know that there was a time when I could have been one of them.

These men and women who once ministered for Christ were initially full of faith as they consecrated their lives to the call of God. At some point in their lives, they probably knelt before God in a Hannah-like moment and said, "God, just use me; I'll go where you want me to go; I'll say what you want me to say; I'll do what you want me to do." Out of devotion to Christ, they wanted to spread the gospel and see people experience salvation through Jesus.

But somewhere along the way that didn't happen, and now they are leaving the ministry to work elsewhere. Today, 1,500 ministers leave the ministry each month because of contention in their churches, spiritual burnout, or moral failure.[12] That's roughly one per state per day. Other studies show that 80 percent of seminary graduates who enter the ministry will leave within five years and that 50 percent of pastors who are currently in the ministry are so discouraged they would leave if they could get another job.[13] Imagine the depth of the discouragement that's out there! I can assure you that it's not the stress of getting three points and a conclusion for Sunday's sermon that is driving them to such discouragement.

Pastors are living with the frustration of not experiencing God's blessing on their churches nor seeing growth in the lives of their members. I have a special burden for these pastors because of all the discouragements I have experienced and mistakes I have made. If the shepherd is discouraged or defeated in spirit, his flock will be negatively affected too.

## But Paul's Encouragement Came from God

Yet we aren't the only ones who have faced discouragement. Early Christians not only faced setbacks and disappointments, but often feared for their lives. Even Paul, who planted so many churches, needed encouragement to go on. For example, he wrote that when he arrived in Macedonia "there was no rest for us. We faced conflict from every direction, with battles on the outside and fear on the inside." However, he didn't give up. He continued doing the job he was supposed to do, and he found refreshment from heaven. "But God, who encourages those who are discouraged, encouraged us ..." (2 Cor. 7:5 – 6 NLT). Spiritual encouragement for our pastors and leaders is a critical need today.

## We Are Self-Important Leaders

At church conferences it is easy to get caught up in the comparison game. The most frequently asked question is, "How big is your church?" as if a larger church somehow makes us a greater leader. Likewise, many pastors base their self-esteem on their position within the church, the books they've written, the conferences they teach at, or the places where they are invited to speak. Where in the New Testament do we see Jesus impressed with position or human notoriety?

## But Jesus and Paul Are Servant Leaders

As with Israel in Samuel's day, the condition of our churches, families, and nation is tremendously influenced by the mind-set of our leaders. This is an inescapable truth. That's why Paul wrote to Timothy, a pastor, emphasizing what effective leadership should look like. One of his main reminders was to serve with humility the flock God had given Timothy to shepherd.

As leaders, the goal is not to have people serve us, but rather to aim at putting their needs first. Pastors and teachers aren't the VIPs; the folks in the pew are.

Listen to the apostle's style of leadership: "Just as a nursing mother cares for her children, so we cared for you. Because we loved you so much, we were delighted to share with you not only the gospel of God but our lives as well" (1 Thess. 2:7b – 8). Paul goes on to say that he and his fellow ministers worked hard not to be a burden to the people they loved (v. 9). He describes his interactions with them as the way "a father deals with his own children, encouraging, comforting and urging [them] to live lives worthy of God" (vv. 11 – 12).

Imagine watching Paul ministering to the people like a mother nursing her baby or a father encouraging and comforting his children. It's in the same spirit of Jesus washing the disciples' feet.

Contrast those scenes with some of our contemporary religious superstars who *demand* ridiculous speaking fees and luxurious hotel accommodations. Which do you think better represents Jesus Christ, whom we are called to proclaim?

## WHAT NOT TO DO

With the current decline in American Christianity, it's obvious that we need God's help in both the pulpit and the pew. I believe that all sincere believers feel the same. And I believe we can make changes, through God's grace, to reverse the trend. But first, let's look at dead ends we must avoid.

Once again, Eli is an example of what not to do. "Now Eli, who was very old, heard about everything his sons were doing to all Israel and how they slept with the women who served at the entrance to the tent of meeting. So he said to them, 'Why do you do such things? I hear from all the people about these wicked deeds of yours'" (1 Sam. 2:22 – 23). Although Eli showed concern, he never put a stop to the wickedness. He merely criticized their horrible behavior. Of course, his sons didn't bother to listen and just continued in their nasty, rebellious ways.

Is it any wonder, then, that the spiritual condition of Israel worsened with time? How could these men lead people into the true worship of God when they were so disconnected from God themselves? It doesn't matter how popular Eli and his sons were with the people; in failing to be faithful to God, they were a moral blight to the nation.

At some point, God couldn't abide this behavior any longer. He spoke to Eli through an unnamed prophet and said, "Why do you honor your sons more than me by fattening yourselves on the choice parts of every offering made by my people Israel?" (1 Sam. 2:29).

> **It doesn't matter how popular Eli and his sons were with the people; in failing to be faithful to God, they were a moral blight to the nation.**

Though Eli tolerated wickedness in spiritual leadership, God didn't. Amazingly, God then *revoked his own promise* that someone from Eli's house would always be high priest. "Therefore the LORD, the God of Israel, declares: 'I promised that members of your family would minister before me forever.' But now the LORD declares: 'Far be it from me! Those who honor me I will honor, but those who despise me will be disdained'" (1 Sam. 2:30). Even positions of service to God can be revoked when the Lord is continually dishonored.

Because Eli and his sons (though in disparate ways) put their own interests above those of God and the welfare of his people, God went against his previous promise and removed Eli's family from the priestly positions they had held for generations. God simply declared his remedy: "I will raise up for myself a faithful priest, who will do according to *what is in my heart and mind*" (1 Sam. 2:35a).

Throughout the history of the Christian church, there have always been sleepy, out-of-touch leaders like Eli and scoundrels like his sons who greedily exploit people. And until Christ returns, that will continue to be.

But that doesn't have to be me.

And it doesn't have to be you.

We can put others first and not ourselves.

We can choose, by God's grace, to do what is right in the sight of the Lord.

God wants leaders who see men and women as he does — with compassionate love. Servant leaders who love the people they serve. That's why God appointed Hannah's son, Samuel, to replace Eli and his sons. Samuel had a tender, shepherd-like concern for his people and was in tune with God's purpose for Israel.

Suffice it to say that today God is looking for the same. Ministers, pastors, and believers in Jesus who share his mind and heart and will act accordingly.

He wants his followers to serve as he did — in love.

## DO WE LEAD FROM LOVE OR SELF-INTEREST?

The basic problem in Shiloh was that leaders loved themselves more than they loved the people and more than they loved God. Instead of feeding, guiding, and protecting God's people, Eli and his sons had lost out with the Lord and, as a result, ended up caring little about others.

I believe a similar attitude is spreading in some places across the church. The missing ingredient in so much of our religious activity is sincere sacrificial love for others. We are self-centered and making it all about us. But how can we effectively represent Christ, who in sacrificial love gave his life for others, if we don't deeply care about those he died for? And since "God is love" (1 John 4:8), doesn't it follow that the one great distinguishing characteristic of Christians everywhere should be a self-sacrificing love for people? Doctrine, apologetics, spiritual gifts, and prophecy charts are all great, but God *is* love. Without love, everything becomes meaningless (1 Cor. 13).

The greatest saint we know of revealed his love in a letter to a church he pioneered: "I thank my God *every time I remember you.*" ... "I have you in my heart".... "God can testify how I long for all of you with the *affection of Christ Jesus*" (Phil. 1:3, 7 – 8).

Wow! This sounds like a man who just fell madly in love with a woman and can't get her out of his mind. Paul never learned, thankfully, the contemporary CEO approach to leadership. He valued the fervent love of Christ for people over the aloof corporate approach to ministry that knows little of weeping for and praying over wounded people.

I learned years ago that the time I spend directly ministering to hurting people in my church not only encourages them but also helps me. It stirs my heart with compassion. It energizes my soul. My preaching becomes more effective. And when people know you love and care about them, you can speak difficult truth and they will receive it.

## LOVE GOD, LOVE HIS PEOPLE

One of the practical ways I have found to love people is by sometimes going to our Tuesday night prayer meetings before it begins. Some of our Prayer Band people and deacons do this also. The doors open at 5:00 p.m., so there can be a long line down the middle aisle well before 7:00, when the service officially begins. One by one, people come up with a desire for someone to agree with them in prayer.

When they come to me, I won't let them immediately share their need. Instead, I ask them questions. Through our conversation, I learn a lot about the person. Maybe they are highly educated, or perhaps they are a high school dropout. I learn where they live, how long they have been a believer, where they work, and more. Then I ask about the request they have or the discouragement they're facing. I start to understand the world they live in and the things that keep them awake at night.

Recently, a bright, well-spoken woman in her thirties, whom I will call Pauline, came in for prayer. After we chatted a moment, I asked for her prayer request.

"I'm out of work right now," she said softly.

"What do you do?"

"I'm a medical technician." She was shy and nervous as she continued. "While I was working, I went to night school to take more courses so I could advance my skills, but then I got laid off. Now I'm in debt."

I could tell something else was troubling her. I tried to look her in the eyes, but she avoided eye contact.

"Where do you live?" I asked.

"In Brooklyn."

"I see." She looked away and mumbled. So I tried again, "Pauline, look at me. Where are you living?"

"I'm in Brooklyn."

"A house or an apartment?"

"No, in a shelter," she whispered with tears filling her eyes.

Pauline was ashamed that after having been educated and having a good job in the medical field, she *still* somehow ended up in a homeless shelter. I never would have known if I hadn't stopped to talk to her before we prayed. She is not alone. In New York City many people wonder, "How many paychecks am I away from living in a shelter?" Homelessness is a real possibility for people where I live.

I held Pauline's hands, and as we prayed together, I wept like a baby. Not only did I want God to meet her needs, but I cried because I realized how I needed more wisdom and grace to be a better pastor to her. This woman was bravely facing tough challenges. And here she was attending church each Sunday, seeking encouragement from God's Word. The last thing she needed was a lifeless service and a mechanical sermon. "Lord, have mercy on me."

> **Praying with hurting people helps me to keep the main thing the main thing. And it will help all of us in representing Jesus the way we should.**

To be honest, after praying with people like Pauline, I'm sometimes drained before the meeting even begins. But I'm also challenged by what I've heard. Praying with hurting people helps me to keep the main thing the main thing. And it will help all of us in representing Jesus the way we should.

I often review a personal spiritual checklist before I preach. Why are you up there, Jim? Are you giving good spiritual food to the people Christ died for? Do you truly care about them, or is this a performance so that people might say, "Wow, what a great speaker, or what an excellent pastor"?

This checklist helps to remind me that I am called to love over everything else that I do.

## GOD HELPS US TO LOVE OTHERS

Not every Christian experiences that kind of love all the time. But as we are exposed to the needs of our people and turn to God for help, the love of God will fill our hearts. Love always goes out to the object it loves. When the love of God is controlling us, we will start reaching out to others in ways we have never imagined.

Paul writes that it is the Lord himself who makes our "love increase and overflow for each other and for everyone else" (1 Thess. 3:12). Notice that his love in us can grow and should not remain static. It must also increase beyond the bounds of our church and extend to "everyone else" — and that means even people who mock our faith in Christ.

In Hebrews 6:10 we see: "God is not unjust; he will not forget your work and the love you have shown him as you have helped his people and continue to help them."

Did you see the change in the object there? "He will not forget your *work* and the *love* you have shown him." How do you show your love to God? "As you have helped his people"!

Show me someone who cares about God's people, and I will show you someone who loves God. Show me someone who says they deeply love God but has little concern for his people, and I will show you someone spiritually delusional.

Recently a pastor asked for some advice. "Jim, I love God; I love to spend time with him. But I just can't stand being with people."

Now there's a problem!

"Do you know the best way to show love to God?" I asked. "Just love his people and help them."

We express love to God by being a sister, a brother, a helpful friend to someone else. People who really love us love our children and grandchildren. When they are kind to our offspring, they are often really showing how much they care for us.

This was the tragedy in Shiloh with Eli and his sons. They were in leadership all right, but they didn't see people the way God saw them. They didn't *feel* what God felt.

## CHANGE STARTS WITH ME

We pastors often complain about the lack of spiritual maturity and enthusiasm among our congregations. But for the most part, isn't this just a reflection of the pastor's ministry and heart? If we teach the truth as it is in Jesus and lead in love, won't the people eventually break through into God? If leaders are zealous to "do the work of an evangelist" (2 Tim. 4:5) and have deep compassion for those who don't know Christ, won't their congregations also be influenced to lovingly share the gospel?

It is very rare, when you look through church history, that a church can rise above its leadership. You wish that were not so (and, of course, God can do anything), but in most cases, the temperature of the shepherd is the determining factor on how the sheep live. Faulty shepherds produce unhealthy flocks. That is why God sadly declares through the prophet, "Woe to the shepherds" (Jer. 23:1), and not woe to the sheep!

Now, I'm not one to judge anyone else, because I haven't been a very good shepherd in so many ways. When I began pastoring, my main objective was to just survive and get through the service. I had little concern for the people listening to me — what they were going through and how God wanted to help them. I was self-conscious more than God-conscious or people-conscious. Their approval of my sermon was more important to me than whether they had been helped by the Lord and grown spiritually. How sad!

When I think of all the sermons I have preached in years past with little compassion and love for the people, I have deep regret. I wasn't seeing them the way God sees them. What poor billboards we are for Jesus when we are strangers to the love that gave Christ for the sins of the world.

God's message is one of grace and love, and we are his only representatives here on earth. We must devote ourselves to serving others in love if we want to see God's church expand and prosper. In fact, love for others is *the* unmistakable sign of true spiritual renewal. We Christians, but especially those in leadership, need to examine not only how much we know of the Bible, but how much we love others. God *is* love. How often has our teaching about holiness, heaven, or hell (among other subjects) been doctrinally correct but so loveless it leaves everyone cold?

You don't have to be a pastor in the pulpit to lead in love and shine a light into the darkness of life's storms. You can be a leader in your church, your community, or your home. Avril is a great example of someone who leads in love both inside and outside of her church. She didn't set out to be a leader of a ministry, but God used her compassion and love for the homeless to spread his love in a tangible way — through home furnishings for the impoverished. And God can use each of us to do the same through our own situation and talents. All we have to do is say "yes" to the light and the love of Jesus.

# Chapter 6

# WIND AND FIRE

Experiencing the Power of the Holy Spirit

For a young boy who spent summers playing on hot concrete play-grounds and finding shade in the shadows of the surrounding Brooklyn apartment buildings, nothing was more exciting than a visit to the country. Each summer I would spend a few weeks with my cousins in Milford, Connecticut. This is where Uncle Ed and Aunt May lived. Driving up the gravel road that led to their house on the hill felt as foreign to me as the Northwest Passage. As much as I enjoyed myself, the whole experience was so different from what I knew growing up in Brooklyn.

At night I slept on a cot in their spacious garage. We didn't have garages where I lived in Brooklyn. I also wasn't used to the smell of fresh country air and the feeling of the early morning dew when I walked barefoot on the grass. The rash I developed after playing in the vast wooded areas that surrounded their property was com-pletely foreign to me. How was I supposed to know what poison ivy is? It wasn't a problem on the cement pavement of Parkside Avenue in Brooklyn.

However, I *was* used to going to church on Sunday, and my aunt and uncle took me faithfully to their small church in Milford. There they sang some of the same hymns, an offering was collected, and a sermon was preached, just as at my parents' church.

One Sunday night there was a very special service in that little church. I can't recall the sermon preached, but toward the end of the meeting, the altar area was opened for the people to come forward to worship, sing, and pray. Sitting in the pew, I couldn't see what was happening, but suddenly I felt something that seemed to fill the room. Even my ornery little heart knew something unusual was taking place, and though it was invisible like the wind, I knew it was real.

**While the Holy Spirit may not come to us in wind and fire, we can still experience the stirring power of his presence today.**

After a few minutes, I whispered to my Aunt May, who sat in the pew next to me, "What's happening?"

"Oh, Jimmy, that's the presence of the Lord," she said. "Sometimes he comes quietly; sometimes he stirs us to praise out loud. It's never the same, but what you're feeling is the presence of God."

As soon as she said it, I knew that what she was saying was true. No one could manufacture or whip up what I was sensing. Though I couldn't use my five senses to touch him, God's presence was palpably real in that moment. Time seemed to stop while I basked in the sweetness of Jesus and the greatness of God.

I was young at the time, but decades later as I write these words, I vividly remember that Holy Spirit-filled moment. Scripture calls these moments "times of refreshing ... from the presence of the Lord" (Acts 3:19 NKJV). Over the centuries, countless Christians have experienced what the Psalmist declared: "You will fill me with joy in your presence" (Ps. 16:11). On Pentecost, the disciples experienced that holy presence with a violent wind and tongues of fire (Acts 2:2–4). While the Holy Spirit may not come to us in wind and fire, we can still experience the stirring power of his presence today.

## MAKING ROOM FOR THE SPIRIT

As I grew older and drifted away from the Lord and the church, the memory of that day and others like it stayed with me. They often reminded me of the reality of Christ and the awe I experienced sitting in God's presence.

When is the last time you experienced the reality of God's presence?

Our days are often so hectic that I'm afraid we don't much find time to seek after the Lord's presence. After hitting the snooze button too many times, we crawl out of bed, and we're late before we even get started. The rest of the day is spent catching up, getting things done, and crossing them off our to-do list. By the end of the day, our bodies and minds are exhausted. But little attention has been given to our spiritual side.

You would think, then, that when we attend church on Sunday, we would look forward to enjoying time in God's presence. Unfortunately, our church services are often as overscheduled as we are.

Not long ago, I was speaking at a large church, and I was waiting in the green room for the evening service to start. The people in charge handed me a copy of their run sheet — basically a schedule of what would happen when, and who was supposed to do it. The leader then reviewed it with all of us in the room.

"Okay, the praise and worship will take fifteen minutes. We'll follow with a missions video that runs for four minutes and forty seconds. The soloist will sing for four minutes and ten seconds, and then we'll have announcements for two and a half minutes. After that, we'll proceed with prayer for the offering. Bob, make sure you don't pray more than a minute because last time you went a little long and we only have six minutes to collect the offering before Pastor Cymbala's introduction."

Bob took out a pen and made a note on his copy of the script.

The leader turned to me and said, "After the offering, John will introduce you for ninety seconds, and then you'll have twenty-five minutes to speak."

"For the sake of time, why not skip my introduction and just use one sentence?" I offered.

"No, no, no. We can't do that! It's all written out right here," the leader said, pointing at his copy of the run sheet.

"Well, is it okay if I lead the people in a time of prayer when I finish?"

"No, we've got the choir singing a patriotic medley after you finish."

It wasn't so much the tightly wound service that struck me as odd;

that's commonplace nowadays. It was the prayer the leader offered after he finished going over the schedule.

"Oh, Spirit of God," he said, "come and move among us with blessing and power. Have your way as we yield ourselves to you."

The Spirit moving among us? Yielding to him? Even God would have a difficult time breaking into that tight schedule! Sure enough, the service went off without a hitch. The run sheet was followed exactly. And although we had a meeting, I doubt whether too many had a meeting with God.

I recently told that story to a group of pastors in Pittsburgh. Their nervous laughter told me it was the way things were run in their churches. Why do we do this? As Americans, we already have overly busy days; why would we add that pressure to our church services too?

I think I know why, but few want to talk about it.

The reason so many pastors micromanage and streamline their Sunday service is to keep it moving. No one wants people leaving their services saying that they ran "too long." Church leaders clearly understand that brevity is what most folks are looking for in their church experience. Pastors have found that if they allow the service to occupy too much time, people might not come back. They will find a shorter service somewhere else.

When I discuss this privately with pastors, they acknowledge this. Generally speaking, many attendees are only there because they feel like it's an obligation. As a result, pastors often feel pressured to get their congregation out promptly so they will come back the following week.

You have to keep attendance up, right?

But why are people looking at the clock when they should be enjoying God's Word and presence? If an NFL game goes into overtime, nobody complains. If the movie runs more than two hours, people don't walk out in protest. What is it about church services that gets people antsy? In God's presence, there is supposed to be an abundance of joy. Spending time with him is exactly the thing that recharges our spiritual batteries to face life's challenges. Why are we so eager to leave his presence?

Unless, of course, his presence isn't being experienced.

To those believers who can't wait to run out the door when the benediction is given, I ask, what are you going to do in heaven? There are no video games, football games, smartphones for texting, or Facebook in heaven. There is only God and his presence. If we don't relish time in his presence once a week on Sunday, how do we expect to enjoy eternity with him?

The truth is that in too many churches, people don't experience God's presence. The Sunday services are monotonous and predictable. Or theatrical and human-centered. Many are relieved when it's over so they can move on to more important or more fun things.

Sadly, I have learned that even many church leaders themselves have never experienced the awesomeness of God's presence. All they know about is how to "do church." They are basically "technicians" who know how to keep it "moving," upbeat, funny, and technically impressive with excellence in music. The worship of God is thus reduced to little more than a well-rehearsed production. Time for openness to the Spirit, free-flowing praise or prayer — this is anathema to contemporary church philosophy. To have unscripted time in which the Holy Spirit might manifest himself so that people could actually experience God himself rather than just facts about him is unthinkable! That would take the control out of our hands, and the well-rehearsed production would be ruined.

No wonder so many are leaving the church and Christianity is declining. We don't seem to want God himself to visit us! We would rather have the human than the Divine.

I know the predictable pushback from pastors. "What are we supposed to do? Just sit there and wing it?" Of course not. Spiritual leaders are wise to have a general idea of what they want to accomplish. Teach the Word, sing praises to God, spend time in prayer, and take an offering. But there is something wrong when our services are so tightly programmed and streamlined that there is no openness for the Holy Spirit to interrupt with his agenda. Unless, of course, you don't believe he has one.

> There is something wrong when our services are so tightly programmed and streamlined that there is no openness for the Holy Spirit to interrupt with his agenda.

When we carry on like this, we grieve the Holy Spirit — and he has feelings too.

How can we effectively build Christ's church without the One he sent to help us do it? Isn't the cause behind much of our decline and superficiality the fact that we do not feel the need for the Holy Spirit's power? The reason that most churches do not emphasize prayer is that they neither want nor think they need the Holy Spirit. "We're doing fine without him." Isn't that also why strong prayer for his presence is quite rare? Who we are in Christ and other positional theology has its place, but shouldn't the current sad state of affairs make us desperate for a manifestation of the Holy Spirit?

This is why no strict order of service is outlined in Scripture for the Christian church. In the early church, I'm sure there were things they wanted to see accomplished, but the meeting had to be open enough for the Holy Spirit to lead and direct as he saw fit. We may have sophistication and technology in our services, but those early Christians knew the secret. They were the ones who had visitors leaving their meetings exclaiming, "God is really among you!" (1 Cor. 14:25). I haven't met many leaders who tell me that's what they want to see happen at their church too.

But let's do "real talk," as they say on Fulton Street in downtown Brooklyn. Our culture is no longer a traditional church-going society. Agnosticism and atheism are increasing. If we want to turn back that tide, the Christian community *has* to return to absolute dependence on the Holy Spirit. It was the Spirit who made the early believers such a powerful witness for Christ in the pagan Roman Empire. Are there other options? They knew nothing of what we now call "doing church"; but they grew, and we're shrinking.

## ELI AND SAMUEL IN THE PRESENCE OF THE LORD

If we are not familiar with God's presence, how will we hear him when he speaks? That's the situation that faced Hannah's son Samuel.

After Hannah weaned Samuel, she took him to Eli and offered a prayer of dedication. Then God began the spiritual change Israel so sorely needed. Eli's family went about their business, "but the boy ministered *before the LORD* under Eli the priest" (1 Sam. 2:11). Eli's sons gradually became more corrupt and audacious, but "Samuel grew up in *the presence of the LORD*" (v. 21).

Then one night Samuel heard a voice calling out to him. Thinking it was Eli, the boy ran to him and said, "Here I am, you called me."

But two times, sleepy Eli told Samuel he didn't call him, and he sent Samuel back to bed.

When Samuel came the third time, Eli understood it was the Lord calling Samuel! He told him that if it happened again, he should say, "Speak, LORD, for your servant is listening" (1 Sam. 3:9).

When Samuel again heard his name called, he did as he was told. Then the Lord spoke, telling Samuel about his judgment against Eli's family. Eventually Samuel grew and was recognized as a prophet of the Lord. What the Lord spoke to Samuel was not a new law or doctrine different from that of Moses. God spoke words of warning, direction, and encouragement to Samuel as he spent time in the Lord's presence. The Holy Spirit did the same to Philip, Peter, Paul, and others in the New Testament book of Acts. Those who deny our need of the Holy Spirit's direction and help today because "the canon of Scripture is closed" totally miss the point. It's not new truth or doctrine he brings. We already have God's unchangeable truth in Scriptures, but what we need is the Spirit's life and power!

The timing of God's visitation to young Samuel was pretty incredible. During this era in Israel, there was little evidence of heaven invading earth. "In those days the word of the LORD was rare; there were not many visions" (1 Sam. 3:1). Religion was a predictable, mechanical affair with priests and sacrifices, but little of the living God. Superficial religion was corrupting the nation, but the God of Israel rescued his people and turned things around. He can do it again now for us.

But it must begin with someone, even a boy, becoming acquainted with and treasuring the presence of the Lord. The latter part of the nineteenth century was deeply impacted by the evangelistic efforts of a layperson named D. L. Moody. He became the greatest evangelist of his generation, and his influence still continues today in many ways. How did this uneducated, untrained man without oratorical skills accomplish so much?

According to his own account, he was desperate to win souls for Christ and wasn't experiencing much success. One day while walking down Broadway during a visit to New York City, he experienced the presence of God in such a profound way, he rarely spoke of it afterward because of the sacred nature of that moment. But then everything changed for D. L. Moody. He preached the same sermons, yet people responded in record numbers. His later meetings in Great Britain were so blessed by God that he became a household name among Christians. Like Samuel, it all began with a man experiencing the Living God in a life-transforming experience.

This was not some weird mysticism or emotional excess. Samuel had to experience God's presence for himself, so that he could lead the people back to God. At the time, it was almost unheard of that someone walked close to God, enjoyed communion with him, and understood his heart. This was the change that Israel had been waiting for.

Eli hadn't done this, nor had his two sons. But God eventually judged the three of them — they all died on the same day.

Soon the people knew that Samuel, even as a teenager, walked with God. They began flocking to Shiloh, because they knew the word of the Lord was there, and they wanted to hear from God.

## WE ARE MISSING THE POWER AND PRESENCE

Of course, God is present everywhere, because he's omnipresent. But what Samuel experienced, and what we are missing in our lives and churches today, is the reality of his presence — his manifest presence — something that can be experienced by our spiritual senses as happened when I was a young boy in that church in Milford, Connecticut. The long history of dynamic spiritual revivals is all about the manifest presence of God, when heaven visits earth in a fresh way. Every revival in history began with a person or group of people praying down a new visitation of God's Spirit. When revivals break out, we know that God has reached down in mercy and let us experience him by the Spirit.

> When revivals break out, we know that God has reached down in mercy and let us experience him by the Spirit.

Unfortunately, this longing for the Holy Spirit is foreign to so many of those who are guiding churches and leadership conferences today. In most seminaries, pursuit of the Spirit's blessing is not taught, but rather dismissed as primitive and anti-intellectual. What gives these critics some credibility are the often worked-up, false, or emotional excess of some people in the charismatic movement. In these circles, rather than winning people to Christ, the focus has often been on strange, unbiblical, unedifying manifestations. Others continue a loud (or quiet) emotional atmosphere, thinking they can humanly imitate the Spirit's work. This is a total departure from New Testament teaching. Also, many of the television evangelists and pastors associated with a "Holy Spirit emphasis" are constantly hawking for donations rather than teaching the whole counsel of God. The gullible are taken in, but others use the excesses to justify their rejection of the Spirit's work and presence for today. A true tragedy!

The presence of God was also foreign to Eli and his sons. But didn't they remember the Tent of Meeting that Moses set up in the wilderness hundreds of years earlier when leading the people to the Promised Land? They must have known that Moses went there often to enjoy the presence of God and talk with the Lord as a friend talks to a friend (Ex. 33:11). Surely Eli would also have read about the cloud of God's presence that literally led Israel for forty years on a daily basis. Yet with all that head knowledge and religious history, Eli and his family settled for religion without God—a form of godliness— but strangers to his presence and power.

In Eli's day, God was everywhere (as true today), but his manifest or revealed presence (which usually means his blessing) was absent.

What's worse is that no one seemed to miss it.

There is no escaping that this is where so many of us are at today in both so-called evangelical and charismatic churches.

The choice is clear: Are we content to live without the reality of the presence of God, or will we seek him for the spiritual renewal that will bring grace beyond our wildest dreams and much glory to Christ?

The only answer to a lukewarm church or a struggling Christian is the same as ever—the fire of the Holy Spirit! What else does the Bible teach? Are we going to teach our way out of our current plight? We have a host of interesting teachers, but the church is still shrinking. The evidence of history is irrefutable. When believers humble themselves and pray for more of God, guess what? The Holy Spirit comes! People become convicted of sins they recently justified. Churches receive a new zeal to share Christ, study his Word, and pray. Love abounds in the believing community. And unbelievers come to Christ.

Without the manifest presence of the Holy Spirit, we become spiritually insensitive and are prone to act like the proud Israelites who did what was right in their own eyes.

## ONE EXAMPLE OF LIFE WITHOUT THE SPIRIT

When the Holy Spirit is not leading and controlling believers' lives, some very dangerous trends are sure to develop. At the top of the list must certainly be the current acceptance and even flaunting of social drinking among professing Christians. I'm not talking about the wine with a meal question — that is a personal choice to be made in your own home. I'm referring to the increased use of alcohol — especially hard alcohol — at Christian social events. Consider the following events that have recently been brought to my attention.

A renowned worship leader and composer recently held a concert at which alcoholic drinks were served. One of our members attended and was stunned to see many in the audience holding their glass of beer or liquor while they swayed to the music.

A well-known "church brand" includes an open bar during their baptismal services here in New York City.

A recent Christian men's conference advertised a segment for beer tasting among the scheduled activities.

It seems as if there are no limits to the "I'm not under bondage" attitude of those who feel "victimized" by their more strict upbringings. Hard alcohol is more and more part of the social lives of professing Christians and now is making inroads into church-related events. Of course, it's all embraced and justified by an appeal to grace versus law, along with other anti-legalism arguments. But I sometimes wonder if it's really more about the self-indulgence of people who have lost the sensitivity of the Holy Spirit in their lives.

We are all aware that some believers have turned off lots of people to Christianity and have given Jesus a bad name through their mean spiritual legalism. Religion to them is merely a list of do's and don'ts — mostly don'ts! Emphasis on a spiritual relationship with Jesus and a life of love has somehow escaped them in their pursuit of "holiness." But now the pendulum has swung the other way with a vengeance. The goal for many at this time seems to be pleasing self at all costs, no matter how potentially harmful a habit might be to oneself or as an example to others.

Some have mistakenly maintained that Jesus turned water into grape juice, yet the admonition to "do not get drunk on wine, which leads to debauchery" (Eph. 5:18) reveals the danger of even the common wine consumed in that era and culture.

But we are living in a drastically different day, aren't we? Alcoholism moves across our nation like a deadly blight, harming men, women, teenagers, and worst of all, the fabric of families with small children. The cost to our economy is more than $200 billion, but the human pain and hopelessness associated with alcoholism can't be put into words or statistics. More than 35 percent of all vehicle fatalities in our country are caused by drunk driving.

Some people have an inherent tendency toward the abuse of intoxicants such as liquor. Their first drink can prove to be the first step toward the pain and ruin caused by alcoholism. The road to ruin often begins with one drink — that's all, just one drink. Should they be offered that *first* drink by a believer in Christ?

Many will argue that this is dinosaur-like thinking and not in tune with contemporary realities. Possibly I come across to some as judgmental or self-righteous as I write these warnings. If so, then let me tell you a bit of my story.

My dad was invited to one office party in Manhattan as part of his job at Westinghouse. He took his first social drink there, and it turned out to be the first of thousands of compulsive drinks over the next twenty-two years.

It started with weekend binges when I was only twelve years old. But other changes soon followed. My mother started crying a lot, and I noticed the beatings he gave me came with an intense fury. Soon my dad graduated to drinking every day and night. Eventually it cost him his well-paying job. My mother was advised by her family to leave him, since our home had turned violent. But she hung in there because she feared he would end up in the gutter.

During my teen years, I could never bring friends over to the house, because I never knew what condition my dad would be in. Alcohol made him nasty, violent, and profane in his speech. This was the same father, mind you, who took me to church when I was a child. Only a few close friends knew our secret heartache. My mother endured physical abuse, and I escaped the reality by playing basketball anywhere I could.

My father's behavior affected me in painful ways even as an adult. While I was saying my wedding vows to Carol, my dad was lying drunk somewhere. He did not attend our wedding.

That's what I always think about when I hear people flaunting their so-called "freedom in Christ" or their enlightened view of twenty-first century ethics. One drink at one party did my dad in. And I don't know what weakness lies resident in me. That's why I forgo anything with alcohol content. Not because wine with a meal is wrong, but rather who knows where that drink might lead me? Or someone who watches me drink it?

**Can't we all, regardless of our differing views on what's "lawful," put other people's welfare first?**

Can't we all, regardless of our differing views on what's "lawful," put other people's welfare first? "Therefore let us stop passing judgment on one another. Instead, make up your mind not to *put any stumbling block or obstacle in the way of a brother or sister*" (Rom. 14:13).

Who will God hold responsible for the stumbling blocks put before others for whom Christ died? Are we so narcissistic that we refuse to accept God's clear instruction?

> Let us therefore make every effort to do what leads to peace and to mutual edification. Do not destroy the work of God for the sake of food [or drink]. All food is clean, but it is wrong for a person to eat [or drink] anything that causes someone else to stumble. It is better not to eat meat or drink wine or to do anything else that will cause your brother or sister to fall (Rom. 14:19 – 21).

Can't we give up anything for the greater good of mutual edification? "So whether you eat or drink or whatever you do, do it all for the glory of God" (1 Cor. 10:31). Are these potentially dangerous drinks being consumed for the glory of God? And what about the new convert to Christ who was delivered from a life of partying and excessive drinking? Should anything and anybody connected to Jesus provide the temptation back into that lifestyle?

Certainly this new permissiveness toward hard alcohol is a sign that the sensitivity the Holy Spirit produces is on the wane. Why dabble in anything if it can harm others or us so easily? I believe that within two years there will be marijuana joints being smoked at church youth activities. With marijuana already "legal" now in some states, I expect that America overall will approve its use, and many in the church will follow suit. They will justify it by saying, "Don't judge me, I haven't broken any laws" or "Praise God, I am not a legalist like those other folks."

Oh God, send the Holy Spirit upon us in a new way so that we can see things not as we want to, but as they really are!

## WE NEED THE HOLY SPIRIT TO SEE

During a renewal of the Holy Spirit, one of the first things that happens is that our perception of spiritual realities becomes keen. We see this in the story of Samuel. As the boy grew up, he saw things the way God looked at them — even though they were invisible to the human eye. He saw the hearts of people and their spiritual condition; he understood the victory God would bring if the people humbled themselves before him. All of this insight was gained, not through academic training, but through the Spirit of the Lord upon Samuel. His words were weighty, and the Lord "let none … fall to the ground" (1 Sam. 3:19). The Spirit of God attested to his legitimacy and spiritual authority (v. 20), which helped the people to receive his messages. He never once considered what folks *wanted* to hear or how he could get them out the door promptly so as to get a good table at lunch. No, Samuel spoke as the Lord directed him.

Spirit-filled, Spirit-led ministry always functions in that manner, because the minister is more focused on God's approval, rather than the audience's response, applause, or attendance figures.

Young Samuel seemed to be the only one in Shiloh who enjoyed and coveted the presence of God. Eli and his sons were carrying on happily without the Spirit's blessing, and in so many ways that describes what is often happening among us today. We have churches, ministers, and Christians who feel no daily need of the Holy Spirit's presence, guidance, comfort, or strengthening.

In fact, I know there's a slew of ministers who will ridicule what I'm writing now. They are church leaders, not unbelievers. And this is the problem. The deadliest opposition to the Holy Spirit isn't from outside the church; it's from the inside. It's not the secular world making fun of the "holy rollers." That will never stop the church. Let those people say what they want to say. The mighty Roman Empire, which eventually crumbled, arrogantly dismissed the early church; but Christ's church remains. Secular opposition has never been the problem. It's when ministers, leaders, and seminaries reject the Spirit of God as our only source of power.

The Spirit was the secret of the apostles' effectiveness, and that's the way God still wants to do things today.

Now, if someone shows me a clear passage in the Bible that says the Holy Spirit is not supposed to help us today, I am happy to be corrected. I read no such verse in Scripture. Rather, everywhere in the New Testament I read of the church's need of the Holy Spirit! If we are ever going to make an impact on an ungodly, cynical, secular society, how can we do it without the Holy Spirit?

Some schools of biblical interpretation believe in the rapture of the church followed by a time when the Holy Spirit will in some way be taken from Earth.

I am not certain what the last days will look like, but I know that for many churches, the Spirit of God left a long time ago.

Our spiritual forefathers certainly depended on the Spirit's presence and help. And so must we. What will happen to our young people who go from their teens into college and then are inundated at school with anti-Christ, atheistic teaching, if they have no experience with the living God? How will they cling to Christ unless the Holy Spirit is working powerfully in their lives and making the Word of God real to them? As everyone is aware, sincere teaching on biblical principles and morality alone is not doing the job. Just look around and decide whether or not we need a visitation of God's presence.

**If pastors preach with the passion that comes from being with Christ, won't the audience fall more in love with the Lord?**

As a wise person once said concerning spiritual truth, "If it's new, it's not true; if it's true, it's not new." Yet there remains a continual human fascination with the newest and trendiest thing out there. That's fine with cell phones, but it doesn't apply to doing the Lord's work.

Perhaps this is a reminder that we often must go backward to move forward. If we want to experience sorely needed blessings from God, we must return to the old pathways of seeking God's Spirit and avoid the "new" that is not ultimately true.

I know our need of the Spirit as we face daily challenges in downtown Brooklyn. Inner-city youth often live with little parental guidance, lack a dad in the house, attend schools with metal detectors, encounter vicious gangs recruiting for new members, and deal with peer pressure to wear the latest $150 sneakers. Kids often seethe with anger and have high walls of resentment up around them. They need the gospel of Jesus and a life-changing experience with the Holy Spirit. What else will deliver them from a wasted life and a lost soul?

If unbelievers of all ages experience the power and love of a Holy God, are they not more likely to turn to Jesus and away from their sin?

And if pastors preach with the passion that comes from being with Christ, won't the audience fall more in love with the Lord?

## THE HOLY SPIRIT CHANGES THE PULPIT

One of the beautiful results of the Holy Spirit's blessing is a changed pulpit with more powerful preaching. Today we suffer from a distinct lack of the prophetic when it comes to preaching. I am not referring to foretelling future events (a type of prophecy), but rather the Spirit-given insight to apply God's Word and heart into a given situation — a "forth telling." We need more than just a clinical dissection of what the words of Scripture mean. We need both Word *and* Spirit.

Without seeming unkind, I must observe that too many of us pastors are satisfied to preach and lead church services without craving the Spirit's help and blessing. And most Christians are not seeking the Spirit's help daily to live victoriously and share their faith with boldness.

I recently picked up one of the latest Christian books on how to be a more effective speaker. In the entire two hundred pages, there was hardly a reference to the person and work of the Spirit. The book was by a prominent guru on how to communicate in the twenty-first century. Afterward, I thought, "What Bible does he read? Has he never read the promises of Jesus connected to the Holy Spirit?" There was a whole chapter on the effective use of PowerPoint, but not one on our vital need of the presence of the Lord to build Christ's church. Other leaders, especially younger ones, will devour these "keys" with the inevitable results predicted by Jesus: "apart from me you can do nothing" (John 15:5).

Could it be that we have "grieved" (Eph. 4:30) and "quenched" (1 Thess. 5:19) the Holy Spirit by neglect and human pride to the point that his presence and blessing are fast disappearing from American churches?

Contrast this attitude with that of Moses, who told God that if his presence didn't accompany the Israelites, he would not move from where he was, since that was what made them special — God's manifest Presence with them (Ex. 33:15).

Everyone knows that a church must have a strong pulpit and strong preaching. And believers are supposed to be daily spreading the message with boldness. For two thousand years it has been the Christian witness of men and women, helped by the Holy Spirit, that has brought people to salvation. Others have helped straying believers back to God. *But all this is utterly impossible without the enablement of the Holy Spirit.*

Likewise, we must remember that the Holy Spirit was sent to glorify Christ and him alone. The minute any speaker wants to see himself glorified and enlarge his ego, wants his local church to be lifted up as something special, or has a denominational banner that he wants flying high, he grieves the Spirit. Whenever we want to glory in anything other than Jesus, no matter how subtly that might happen, the Holy Spirit withdraws his influences — sometimes very dramatically.

It's as if the Holy Spirit says, "No, I will not help you do that. I was only sent to glorify Christ and build up his church. If you want to glorify yourself, if you want your denominational name to be in bold print, if you want people to know they're attending a really important church, that is not my mission. You're on your own; go for it. I was sent to exhibit my power and grace only on those who proclaim the good news of Jesus and glorify Christ."

We need to pray that our church workers — whether teaching a children's class, leading a choir, or preaching a sermon — will lift up only Christ and his gospel, so that the Holy Spirit will help them. If other motives are mixed in, we are all going to suffer. Christianity is weakening as a force in society — of that there is no question. We need to root for and pray that all Christians will have the Spirit of God blessing their labors.

When the Spirit of Christ is grieved and his "fire" put out, we are predominantly left with the human element and little sense of the awe of God. As with Israel, we can be defeated in battles we should be winning.

We have more technology and talent at our disposal today than we have ever had before. Has it proven to be the answer?

We have less and less of God's blessing and presence among us.

Do we not need more?

We need less of us and more of him.

## WHAT DOES IT LOOK LIKE TO GLORIFY CHRIST?

A few weeks ago, at the last minute my wife, Carol, asked her assistant to fill in to lead the noon worship service. This man regularly leads us in worship, but he was not particularly prepared for this occasion, yet he obliged Carol. As he led worship, he didn't say much; he just led the congregation in singing and worshiping God. As worship leader, he certainly wasn't the focal point. People could hear themselves and others singing.

As the congregation ended one of the praise songs, there was a pause. No one jumped in immediately to fill it. Instead, the people were allowed to bask in the moment as they vocalized their praise to God.

In that moment, the people began gradually to worship God more freely and louder. Many raised their hands, as all got lost in praising God in Spirit and in truth. It seemed that while thousands audibly worshiped, no one single voice was heard — only the combined voices of a new Spirit-formed choir praising Jesus.

Carol walked to the microphone and said, "The Lord is here. Let's all worship him."

Immediately, there was a louder swell of voices in English, Spanish, Creole, and who knows what else. Others just worshiped through tears. As the more than three thousand people in the auditorium and hundreds more in the overflow room freely worshiped God, one could sense his Spirit among us. God was so real and precious that I wept for joy. Visitors and members alike were lost in the moment of praise and glory to God.

No leader was leading the service.

No one was following the run sheet and counting the minutes until the next scheduled item.

The Holy Spirit had taken over the meeting.

The people were doing what they were created for. Each person worshiped and prayed as they desired. We didn't plan for it, but when it happened, we allowed it. This precious time lasted for about fifteen minutes. An offering was taken later, the choir sang, and a sermon was preached, but when it was all done, the lingering sense of God's presence stayed with all of us.

> Christians might hear their faith mocked in the marketplace daily, but experiencing God the Holy Spirit will never leave them. It only creates a hunger for more.

My instincts were confirmed when, after the service, out-of-town visitors stopped me in the hall and told me how awed they were by the presence of God. No one looked at their watches, and no one got up to leave early. Many said that they wanted more of what they experienced that afternoon. As they talked about their experiences in that service, it reminded me of that Sunday night in Milford.

Christians might hear their faith mocked in the marketplace daily, but experiencing God the Holy Spirit will never leave them. It only creates a hunger for more. We need to invite the Spirit into our churches and make room for him in our lives throughout the week. When he comes, he makes Jesus Christ real and strengthens us to face every difficult challenge before us.

# Chapter 7

# INTO THE DARKEST NIGHT

Bethsaida's Story

*As a child, Bethsaida grew up attending Brooklyn Tabernacle, but like many youth, when she became a teenager she rebelled, stopped coming to church, and turned her back on her faith. Fortunately, she had experienced the Lord so that during her time of rebellion, she couldn't escape his love. Hearing his kind and gentle whisper was the prompting she needed to turn her life back to God. Bethsaida then faithfully served the Lord for years, appreciating the Bible in a new way and serving others with unusual grace.*

*Soon after, out of nowhere, the Holy Spirit deposited a burden in her for women and girls who are being trafficked. She has since gone all over the world ministering to those who are ensnared in this despicable crime. Bethsaida understands the pain and humiliation these women feel, and she believes that intervention is necessary to set them free. She also knows human efforts alone won't solve the problem. So she and others at our church recently started prayer meetings at which hundreds of people gather just to pray against this monstrous evil.*

*Bethsaida has depended on that kind of intercessory prayer and the promptings of the Holy Spirit when she walks along foreign beaches or enters nightclubs to meet with young girls involved in sex trafficking. In those shadowy and dangerous places, she listens for the voice of the*

*Holy Spirit to direct her to those she should talk to, what she should say,*
*and how to say it. Even in the most unlikely places, Bethsaida knows*
*the Lord will guide her. She is confident she will hear his promptings*
*even in a noisy nightclub with pulsating lights and loud music.*

*Why is she so confident?*

*I will let her tell you.*

## BETHSAIDA

I like to tell people I started going to church nine months before I was born, and my mother gave birth to me in a pew. While that is an exaggeration, I felt like when I was growing up we were *always* at church.

Long before I was born, my mother divorced her first husband and moved to a small apartment in Brooklyn with my sister. My sister was the first to get saved, and my mom quickly followed. Eventually my mother caught the eye of an usher at the church. Not long after they were married, they had me and my brother. So we had good reasons for always being at church. I can't remember my life without the Brooklyn Tabernacle being at the center of it.

One memory from those early days stands out, though. I was five years old and attending our Kiddie Church one Sunday. The teacher asked us to raise our hands if we wanted to accept Jesus into our hearts. I raised mine. Of course I wanted more of Jesus! The teacher took those of us who responded to the back of the room and had us sit down on the steps. There we prayed a prayer of salvation. Whenever I think about that day, it's like an out-of-body experience — I look back on that moment and see myself sitting on the steps, head bowed, praying with my teacher.

Growing up, I always wanted to help people, so it was natural for me to want to tell them about Jesus; in fact, it was a joy for me to do that. I loved to sing, and there was nothing better than singing for Jesus, so I joined the youth choir. When people asked me what I wanted to be when I grew up, I didn't have a specific career goal in mind, but I always said, "I want to do music and help people." I wanted to combine those two things at church by volunteering for the toddler ministry; unfortunately, they thought I was too young.

I was only ten at the time.

At home, my parents were very protective. My father was a New York City sergeant, and over the years, I'm sure he's seen a lot of bad things. To keep us safe, my parents enrolled us in a private Christian school and did their best to protect us at home by eliminating influences they thought would harm us. We weren't allowed to listen to secular music or watch the Smurfs on television. Today I am thankful for my godly parents, but when I was fourteen, I felt like a prisoner in my own home.

When I entered high school, I began to rebel and do my own thing. I was drinking, dating guys who weren't good for me, and fighting constantly with my dad. My independent spirit and my father's protective nature caused a lot of tension in our home. But a deeper problem existed between us.

My father worked hard to provide for us, and he showed his love by making sure we never lacked anything. But I never heard, "I'm proud of you," or "You're beautiful," or anything like that from him. Once, I remember bringing home a report card with a bunch of As and one C. Instead of praising me for the As, he questioned me about the C. Conversations like that caused me to grow bitter toward him. I just wanted him to be proud of me. I didn't want him telling me what to do or how to do it.

More than anything, I needed him to demonstrate his love to me in ways that, as a teenager, I could understand. I wanted him to be more affectionate, to hug me, kiss me, or encourage me with his words. I wanted him to tell me I was beautiful and worthy to be loved. I didn't understand that the way he showed his love was by providing for us. As a young girl struggling to grow up, I made poor choices based on what I perceived as my father's lack of affection.

Out of my bitterness, I adopted an ultra-feminist attitude. At the same time I was craving love and encouragement from a man, I determined that my identity would not be found in one. If I dated one guy, I dated a bunch of guys. I never wanted to be attached to just one and be dependent on him for all of my needs.

During this time of rebellion, I turned my back on God. My personality is pretty much all or nothing. So, unlike some of my friends who slid away from their faith but continued to attend church, I just stopped going altogether. I stopped singing in the choir and started going out to clubs. I had nothing to hide; this was who I was.

When I was eighteen years old, I was hanging out in a club one night doing a bunch of things I shouldn't be doing. The room was dark, lit only by a steady blue light on the dance floor. The music was fast paced and heavy on the bass. *Boom, boom, boom.* The place was packed with people. In a surreal out-of-body experience, I remember looking around the crowded room. Everywhere I looked I could see people who were messed up. Guys were lying on the floor, obviously strung out. A crowd of people gyrated on the dance floor. But I could tell from the looks on their faces and the fact they had a hard time keeping their balance that most of them were out of it. What would have been obvious to anyone else suddenly came as a revelation to me — everyone in the place was either drunk or high on drugs!

> **Somewhere inside of me I recognized the voice of the Holy Spirit, and I knew that what he said was right and true.**
>
> *— Bethsaida*

While I observed them from a distance, I heard a voice. It was kind but firm, like a person speaking with authority, only it wasn't an audible voice; it seemed to be a voice from within me. It felt as if it came from my heart, but it was somehow separate from me. "You don't belong here," the voice said. But it wasn't condemning. It was very gentle.

It's true, I thought.

Somewhere inside of me I recognized the voice of the Holy Spirit, and I knew that what he said was right and true.

Though it wasn't enough to get me to change my ways and go back to the Lord, that experience stayed with me. From then on, when I hung out in a club, I would think, *I don't belong here.*

A few weeks later, my girlfriends and I went clubbing on a bar-lined street. We randomly picked one, and we were hanging out inside when suddenly we heard a lot of sirens. Fire trucks pulled up to one of the bars just a few buildings away from where we stood. We watched as the firemen rushed inside and the bar patrons rushed out. An eyewitness told us a man had walked into that bar and thrown kerosene. He planned to light it before someone stopped him.

I was shocked. I could have been in that bar. We could have just as easily picked that one as we did the place where we were. It got me thinking. *What if he had picked the same bar I was in? What if he had lit this place on fire, and I died? What if I had to face God? What would I say?*

I knew the things I was caught up in were wrong, but I justified it by saying I wasn't as bad as my friends. I was still a "good girl." But the experience got me thinking. My first reaction was to think of meeting God ... but was there really a *God*?

I had been struggling with these questions ever since I heard the voice in the club. I knew my parents loved the Lord. And growing up in the church, I could see that Pastor Cymbala and so many others there loved the Lord. But I didn't want to follow Jesus just because they did. I wanted to know if God was real and true. My independent nature wanted to know if he was worth following. Or was he someone else who would disappoint me?

From my experiences growing up, I knew God could provide for me — my earthly dad demonstrated that. But I faced a deeper question. *Could God love me?*

The thought of coming face-to-face with God in the club left me feeling as if I wasn't good enough. Standing and looking at the fire trucks at the club down the street, I was afraid that if I met God that night, he would have been disappointed in me and my actions. I needed someone who loved and valued me, and now I was afraid that God didn't.

That same summer I was eighteen, I spent time in Florida with my uncle, who is a pastor. One Sunday he preached a message about how Moses didn't feel as if he was good enough to be used by God. That sermon touched my heart. I had recently become more convicted of my sins. I knew what I had been doing was wrong. But now I wondered, if God was real, and if I came back to him, would he ever want to use me after I'd messed up so much?

In church that day, I silently prayed. "God, I've messed up so much. I don't know how you could love me or use me. I'm too far gone for that, but if you ever could, please take what I have. It's not much, but if you can use it, take it."

When I got back to New York, I still went to the clubs, but not as often as I had before. I did, however, make other changes. I started attending a new church, occasionally at first and then more regularly. I didn't want to go back to Brooklyn Tab; I just wanted to try something new, in a new environment, and start over again. But the nagging questions remained. *Is God real? Does he love me? Is he the person I should follow?*

It was hard being filled with questions and doubts in a church where I didn't know anyone. At Brooklyn Tab, there were hundreds of people who knew my family, and I could have talked to any one of them, but in the new church I felt alone with my doubts. I decided the answer was to meet more people and get involved as I had been at Brooklyn Tabernacle. When an audition for the Christmas play was announced, I decided to try out. This would give me an opportunity to meet and get to know a lot of people. Maybe getting more involved would help to answer some of my questions.

The audition was on a Monday night, and I showed up early, filled out the paperwork, and sat in the pew to wait my turn. Soon, more people came and filled in the space next to me. The pews in front of and behind me were filled. People surrounded me, yet no one said a word to me. In fact, no one even looked me in the eye or smiled.

Sitting in that sanctuary surrounded by so many Christians laughing and talking, but not to me, I felt the loneliest I have ever felt. It was a deep and intense loneliness, something I can honestly say I hope no other human, even my worst enemy, ever feels. More than ever, I needed someone to love me.

In that moment I wanted to believe God was real and if he were, he was all that I had. So while I sat alone in the crowd, I prayed. *God, if you're real, please prompt someone to smile at me. Maybe someone could say hi to me. Just have someone come up and talk to me.*

It was a sincere prayer straight from my heart. I didn't say it out loud or even move my lips. More than anything, I wanted God to be real, but I needed proof. I felt so alone and broken, and I was desperate for him to show me that he loved me. A smile was all I needed to know that he was real.

But nothing happened.

I wish I could say that as I finished praying, someone came over to speak to me or turned in the pew and smiled at me. But as hard as I looked for proof that God was real, that he heard my prayer, and that he loved me, there was none. No one acknowledged me the entire night, not during the audition, and not even as we got up to leave. While everyone else said their good-byes, I sat there alone.

It was as if I were invisible.

On the way home, I felt distraught. *God, I want to believe you are real, but no one saw me. No one looked at me, said anything to me, or even smiled. I want to believe that you love me, but after tonight, I can't do it. I just can't believe in you.*

I returned home that Monday night, and without saying anything to anyone in my family, I went straight to bed. *What's the point?* I thought. *God isn't real, and if by some chance he is, he obviously doesn't care about me.*

A few days later, on Friday, my sister and her husband came to town for the weekend. They lived in Connecticut, where he pastors a church. They had been at the house a short time when I headed up the steps to my room.

"Hey, Bethsaida, I called you on Monday," my brother-in-law said.

"I was at church auditioning for something," I replied.

"Yeah, your mom told me," he continued, as I started up the stairs. "I called because I was praying, and God told me to stop praying and call you. He wanted me to tell you that he loves you."

My jaw dropped and I gasped. I could feel the hairs on my arms standing on end as I turned toward him. "What? What did you say?"

"I was praying, and the Lord told me to stop praying and call you and tell you that he loves you."

I was stunned. While I was at my lowest moment, God was using my brother-in-law in another state to reach out to me.

I'm a thinker and a doubter, and I battle a lot with my thoughts. Had someone smiled at me at church, I would have second-guessed God by asking, *Is that a coincidence, or did God tell them to smile at me?* But now I saw that God had answered my prayer in a way I couldn't doubt. I hadn't told anyone what had happened on Monday night or how I had prayed. There was no way that my brother-in-law could have known unless God told him. That moment changed my life. I knew then and there that Jesus was real and that he loved me more than I could possibly imagine.

> **I'm a thinker and a doubter, and I battle a lot with my thoughts.... But now I saw that God had answered my prayer in a way I couldn't doubt.**
> *—Bethsaida*

I thought back over the previous five months how he had spoken to me in the club with his kind and gentle voice, how he had nudged me with the sermon that my uncle preached, and how he had used my darkest moment to show me how deep his love is for me. Knowing how much he loved me, my only response was to live my life as a thank you for his love.

In college, I majored in music business. While interning for a music business law firm in 2004, I was flipping through a magazine, and I found an article written by a guy who wrote about how awesome it was to go to the Philippines and buy fourteen-year-old girls for sex. He was encouraging other men to do the same. Reading that article, I remember praying, *Jesus, I want to go to the Philippines and tell these girls how much you love them, that you value them, and how precious they are to you. I want to tell them they don't need a man to give them their identity; they can find that in you.*

It was an unusual prayer for me because I was born and raised in Brooklyn. I hardly traveled, and there was no way I would ever make it to the Philippines. I put that thought on the back burner.

Though I was serving at church during that time, most of my prayers were pretty me-centered. Thank you for blessing me. Thank you for loving me. Help me find the right job. Help me find the right boyfriend. Help me get a husband. It was all about me, me, me.

When I graduated in 2005, there were no jobs available in the music industry, so I started teaching music in an after-school program, and it was there I learned about a teaching fellows program. I was living for God and trusting him with my life, but I wasn't sure what he wanted me to do. I decided if I got the teaching job, that would be God's will. If not, I would go to Bible school. After struggling with the teaching interview, I was pretty sure I was headed to Bible school, but somehow I got the job anyway. I started teaching in the inner city in Brooklyn in 2007.

At night, I took classes to get my master's degree in education. It was an intense time. I would leave for my job when it was dark, and I would return from school when it was dark. I don't think I saw the sun for a whole year! But I loved the art of teaching, and I loved the kids I taught during the day, so it was all worth it.

I also returned to Brooklyn Tabernacle, where God continued to teach me, and I grew in my faith.

In 2009, God used a Facebook invitation to get my attention. I don't even know who sent it, but it was an invitation to a film screening about something called "human trafficking." I didn't know what it was, but I was drawn to the issue. I attended the screening with some friends, and what I saw rocked my world. That night I learned about modern-day slavery and little girls being abused sexually and getting psychologically destroyed. These girls weren't much older than the fifth graders I was teaching; some were even younger.

I watched the documentary that night, and I made the connection between human trafficking and the article I'd read in the magazine in 2004. I was appalled by what I saw and astounded by the fact that this was going on in our world today. But now, I had a name for it.

God, why hasn't the Christian church not fought against this? What has the church been so consumed with?

The Holy Spirit once again, very gently but very firmly, asked, "What have *you* been so consumed with?"

I thought about all of the me-centered prayers I had been praying and realized that I was part of the church at large that I was blaming. Then I remembered the prayer I prayed while reading the magazine article, and instantly I knew I had to do something about it.

I went home and Googled "human trafficking" and "mission trips." I found something called **The Holy Spirit once again, very gently but very firmly, asked, "What have *you* been so consumed with?"**

The World Race. It is an eleven-month trip around the world. Each month, participants are in a new country, serving under a church or other organization and partnering with them in whatever way they need to be served. It could be painting outhouses, babysitting, preaching door-to-door, or teaching. Participants didn't stay in hotels; they brought a backpack and a tent and lived with the people they served. To a girl from New York City, tenting was about as extreme as it could get. I had never camped before in my life. And I hate bugs! But I felt God calling me to go, so I finished out the teaching year, and in 2010 I left.

During the next eleven months, God taught me a new lesson each month about who I am in him, his love for me, and how I can serve others in his name. My father was a huge support for me in this endeavor. He not only expressed his love for me in many ways, but also showed how proud he was of me. This was a beautiful part of God's healing process for me. It was a humbling experience, and it broke many of the me-centered strongholds in my life. The issue of human trafficking continued to prick my heart, and I continued to pray about what God was asking me to do about it.

In month nine of The World Race, we ended up in the Philippines in a place called Puerto Galera—a stunningly beautiful island. But the evil there contrasted with the beautiful setting. Men would buy girls for the weekend and take them on "vacation" to this island. The girls were called bar girls because they worked in the clubs, which were basically fronts for prostitution. It was such a culture shock to see middle-aged white men holding hands with young Filipino girls and no one batted an eye. Everyone there was just so used to it.

*Oh, my God,* I would cry out inside. *How is everyone okay with this? Look at this horrible thing!* During our time in the Philippines, the leaders of The World Race gave us the freedom to pursue the projects that were on our hearts. So my teammates and I would walk the beaches and talk to the girls, hear their stories of why they were there, what they were doing, and whether they liked it.

None of them did.

One of the conversations I remember most was with a girl named Paris who felt that she wasn't good enough. That God couldn't love her and wouldn't want her because of all of the things she'd done wrong. I shared my story with her and assured her it wasn't true. When I later learned that she left the man who bought her and returned to her family at home, I felt as if God had used us to help her.

During that time, I know God used us to touch many lives, but just as important, he touched mine. A trip to Thailand for The World Race further opened my heart to victims of sex trafficking. When the race ended, I returned to Thailand to work with an organization that did outreach work to women and girls who wanted to leave the sex trade. I spent a year there, where I served under people who spent their lives committed to the issue and learned much about the players involved. It was Satan's playground, so evil and demonic, with people being used left and right. The girls were good actresses, and they always had smiles on their faces. I didn't. I often had tears on mine.

Since then, I have also made another trip to the Philippines, this time to Angeles City, the place I had read about in that magazine article so long ago.

I didn't stay there long. Angeles City was even darker than Thailand—if that's possible. Unlike Thailand, where lots of mission organizations were at work, Angeles City was one of the spiritually darkest places I've ever been. No one seemed concerned for the girls here. There is only one nonprofit Christian organization trying to serve the more than 15,000 girls being trafficked to American and European men during the high season at Christmas.

I was never closer to God than when I was there.

In 2012, God called me back to New York City to take what I learned around the world and apply it to the place where I grew up. I knew from field experience that many girls in foreign countries end up in the sex trade because they are motivated financially to provide for their family. It's different in America.

In New York City, pimps prey upon the girls who are being trafficked because they're vulnerable. Many of them have struggled with the same things I struggled with — loneliness, not feeling beautiful, and not feeling loved.

The darkest times in my life made me sensitive to the needs of these girls. I knew what it felt like to be trapped and stuck. I had experienced deep loneliness and the thought that I was so bad God could never use me again.

But I also experienced the gentle voice of the Holy Spirit calling out to me and saying, "You don't belong here," and prompting my brother-in-law to call me and tell me that God loves me.

I don't know what God has in store for me next, but I do know he has a plan and that he loves me. And that I want to spend my life helping people who are in trouble. I want them to hear the Lord's kind, firm voice saying, "You don't belong here. I love you. And I will work through you."

For a long time I had questioned whether God was real and whether I was worthy of his love, but looking back on my life, I can see God has always been with me and loving me from those earliest days in church at Brooklyn Tab. I may not have been born in the pew, but something was born in my heart in the pew — I heard the still, small voice of the Holy Spirit.

# Chapter 8

# WATCHES AND WARNINGS

## Keeping a Clear Gospel Message

I stood in the conference bookstore signing books when Will Graham, son of Franklin Graham and grandson of Dr. Billy Graham, said, "You need to come with me."

"Sure, just as soon as I finish signing these books." I had been teaching at the Billy Graham Training Center at The Cove, in Ashville, North Carolina, and people who wanted to meet me and buy a book were patiently waiting in line.

"No, you've got to come now. I've already talked to my dad and to my grandfather. Since you are representing the Billy Graham Association at several pastors' events, we think it is important for you to meet him, and for him to meet you as well."

Will had recently been appointed the executive director of the Billy Graham Training Center at The Cove — a good choice, because he is so gifted by God. But he was also a take-charge kind of guy. He turned to the people in line and said, "I'm sorry, but unfortunately, Pastor Cymbala has to leave now. You'll have an opportunity to see him later this evening."

On the ride up to Montreat and the big rustic house where Dr. Graham lived, I thought about all he had done for the kingdom and about his public and private legacy. Our church choir had sung at a few of his crusades, and Carol had met him in passing, but I had never met him.

When we arrived at the house, a group of employees was just finishing a cake-cutting ceremony for an employee who had worked there for twenty years. Through the crowd, I could see Dr. Graham's white hair. He was sitting in his wheelchair, wearing sunglasses. He looked frail, with a small tube in his nose due to a respiratory infection. We sat down as the others left, and Will introduced me, talking loudly, because Dr. Graham's hearing had diminished.

"Hello. How are you?" I said. I'm often reserved when I meet people I don't know, and truthfully, I felt a little uncomfortable. I felt I was an intrusion in the day of an ailing elderly man. I needn't have worried. Will did most of the talking.

"You know, Grandpa Bill, Pastor Cymbala preached a very important message last night. Very, very important for me."

During my message, I had noticed Will furiously taking notes. I didn't think anything I had said was that profound, but if it had helped him in some way, I was thankful.

"What did he preach on?" Dr. Graham asked, turning his head slightly.

"He preached from Mark 3 on our first calling as ministers. Actually, everybody's first calling."

"And what's that?" Dr. Graham asked.

"He preached about Jesus going up on the mountain, and how he called the disciples so they might be with him, so he might send them out to preach, and so they would have authority over evil spirits, but he put emphasis on the fact that the first calling was that they might *be with him*."

This moment was surreal. Will was telling Billy Graham about my sermon!

"And I needed to hear that," Will continued. "Because as an evangelist, and now as the executive director, I'm on the road a lot. Pastor Cymbala said our first calling was not to write books, not to travel, not to do whatever, but it's to be with Jesus. And you know what, Grandpa Bill? I *really* needed that."

Dr. Graham jerked his head up, and his voice cracked. "No," he said, "*I needed* to hear that because I need more of Jesus, and I'm ninety-three!"

Billy Graham is probably the greatest evangelist of our time. He could have responded with, "Yes, I know. I've preached sermons on that, and I've preached them better than Jim Cymbala could!" And we all would have agreed.

Instead, he humbly responded, "No, I needed to hear that."

In that moment, I understood why God had used Billy Graham in such a powerful way. Though I didn't say ten words, God used our conversation to remind me, "That's what I am looking for in my people." It was Dr. Graham's humility in pointing others to Christ and not toward himself that made him such a choice servant of the Lord.

**Keep to a simple gospel message. Only a clear gospel message will help represent Christ in the coming storm.**

Since that visit with Dr. Graham, I have had the opportunity to watch some rebroadcasts of his sermons. Compared to many of the televangelists of today, it's as if he were preaching a different religion! Dr. Graham's message was always simple and to the point. He never drew people to himself, but always to God. He spoke of man's spiritual need and God's provision in sending his Son to die for our sin. Jesus bore the judgment for the sins of the world when he shed his blood on the cross. It's the same gospel that has been preached for two thousand years. When Billy Graham preached, it came from a humble heart that seemed to say, "I need this Jesus as much as you do." It seemed as if a loving God was calling out to sinners through him.

We don't hear that simple message enough today. It seems many modern pastors aren't preaching the same gospel he did, and we are certainly not preaching it with the same humility.

I'm all for using every helpful technology, as long as it accompanies the one unchangeable gospel. But I'm convinced that many have subtly altered the message of Christ. Certainly the low numbers of baptisms, life transformations, and attendance at our churches indicate something is wrong. It seems the more we mess with the message, the worse we seem to do. So I ask the church to watch out for this and to issue a warning: keep to a simple gospel message. Only a clear gospel message will help represent Christ in the coming storm.

## SAMUEL'S MESSAGE

Samuel was born from an impassioned prayer, raised in the tabernacle of the Lord, and heard God calling to him one night. The Bible says, "The LORD was with Samuel as he grew up, and he let none of Samuel's words fall to the ground. And all Israel from Dan to Beersheba recognized that Samuel was attested as a prophet of the LORD.... And Samuel's word came to all Israel" (1 Sam. 3:19–20; 4:1).

Samuel lived in a day when the presence of the Lord was rare, yet he had an impact on the entire nation of Israel. So what was Samuel's message, and why did people suddenly flock to him?

The message came to Samuel as a vision. Like most prophets, he saw it before he said it. In fact, prophets are often referred to as seers. In the case of Samuel, he was a seer (1 Sam. 9:19) who spoke for God concerning the people's obedience to the law God had given Moses. Like other prophets', Samuel's calling was to apply God's moral verdict at any given moment with a specific God-inspired application as to the blessings or judgment coming upon the people. Samuel spoke God's words. They weren't new words; they were just prophetic declarations of God's law of sowing and reaping. All of Israel knew that when the word of the Lord came to Samuel, he was faithful to deliver it without holding back.

For example, when the people asked for a king, Samuel knew it wasn't a good idea. He knew that a king would bring trouble and decline to the nation. But God allowed it as part of his plan. He gave Samuel strong warnings to pass on to the people. So "Samuel told all the words of the LORD to the people who were asking him for a king" (1 Sam. 8:10).

Notice that Samuel told them *all the words* of the Lord, not just some of them. He didn't take words out of context or just pass on some upbeat and inspiring message to keep the people happy. His goal was to turn people back to God in obedience to the law. And he did it without worrying about what they wanted to hear or how he could make it more palatable to them. He told the people what God told him, period.

However, Samuel's message is much different than the message we are to proclaim to the world. Christ hadn't come yet when Samuel lived. But many centuries later, Jesus was born and then died for our sins. Because of that, we are asked to share the good news of Christ that Samuel was never commissioned to preach.

## OUR MESSAGE

So what is the message Christians should be proclaiming to the world? What should we be sharing with our friends and family? What message should our churches be known for?

The answer won't be found in Samuel's words or any other prophet of the Old Testament. Neither is it found in the writings of Moses. The great purpose of God for the last two thousand years has been to save people who have been separated from him by their sin and to see them reconciled back to him. The only message that can accomplish this salvation is the gospel of Jesus Christ — the good news of the cross — where Jesus shed his blood to provide atonement for our sins.

Our message is about God's love for every person on the planet. In his infinite love, God sent his Son — Jesus — to become a sacrifice on the cross, so that men and women can be saved from their sins. The commission that Christ gave all his followers was to reach out to people everywhere with this good news, so that they might believe and receive pardon and then experience the Holy Spirit living in them. This is what it means to see a soul saved — rescued out of darkness into the light. Dead in their trespasses but now alive in Christ. Our mission is to preach Jesus, his cross, resurrection, and future return. But as we do so, we encounter strong adversaries.

## OPPOSITION TO THE MESSAGE

When the battle is for an eternal soul, all the powers of hell itself are unleashed against those sent by Christ to share the gospel. To accomplish our mission, the combined forces of the world, the flesh, and Satan himself must be defeated as they work together with diabolical power. This intense, invisible warfare has been ongoing since before Christ rose from the dead and ascended into heaven. Any honest pastor will tell you, the hardest thing in the world is not increasing attendance, but rather seeing a genuine conversion to Christ.

In light of the relatively small numbers of converts most churches are experiencing nowadays, let us learn from the success of the early Christian church. They witnessed a phenomenal expansion of the kingdom of Christ, and the apostle Paul was probably the most successful missionary of all. Listen to his words as he writes to the church he started in Thessalonica:

> For we know, brothers and sisters loved by God, that he has chosen you, because *our gospel* came to you not simply with words but also with power, with the Holy Spirit and deep conviction.

You know how we lived among you for your sake. You became imitators of us and of the Lord, for you welcomed the message in the midst of severe suffering with the joy given by the Holy Spirit. And so you became a model to all the believers in Macedonia and Achaia. The Lord's message rang out from you not only in Macedonia and Achaia — your faith in God has become known everywhere (1 Thess. 1:4 – 8a).

Wow! Former idolaters who in short order became a spiritual model to Christian believers everywhere!

Notice how the new converts were described: "They tell how you turned to God from idols to serve the living and true God, and to wait for his Son from heaven, whom he raised from the dead — Jesus, who rescues us from the coming wrath" (1 Thess. 1:9b – 10).

Observe the incredible power of the simple gospel message. Men and women turned away from the popular pagan idols of their day to trust in God who gave his Son, Jesus, for them. They not only went to church; their lives had a new center as they humbly served the living and true God. They also made the most of their fleeting days on earth as they waited for God's Son to return to earth — the same Jesus who would rescue them from the coming divine judgment. These believers were the real deal; what a church that was in Thessalonica!

**These believers were the real deal; what a church that was in Thessalonica!**

Besides the unspeakable immorality of "divine" emperors such as Tiberius, Caligula, and Nero, the Roman Empire was permeated everywhere with greed, degeneracy, and a constant pursuit of pleasure at any and all costs. Human life meant nothing, and unwanted babies were discarded the way one would throw out the trash. Innumerable gods were worshiped along with the emperors, and the preaching of any kind of monotheism, whether Judaism or Christianity, could often provoke harsh reprisals. No printed New Testaments, no church buildings, often no legal protection from the courts — this was life in the Roman Empire, and yet the church at Thessalonica prospered!

Notice, however, the subtle — and not so subtle — ways this great church differed from what we consider a great church in America. First, we don't hear any mention of the names of the pastor or gifted teacher. The only name celebrated back then was Jesus Christ! If we want to see God's grace defeat the storm facing us, we also would do well to focus less on "super preachers" and give all our attention and the glory to Jesus only.

This was similar to the start of the church in Antioch, Syria, where Paul had been sent out on his missionary journeys. Some unnamed men from Cyprus and Cyrene preached the gospel there, and "the Lord's hand was with them" (Acts 11:20 – 21). The result was one of the great Christian churches in the New Testament, yet we don't even know who founded it. If we desire the "hand of God" (i.e., his power) to return to our churches, we should focus less on the personalities and abilities of people, and more on Jesus and the power of the Holy Spirit.

Notice also that no mention is made of how many people were attending the church in Thessalonica. No public church buildings for Christians to gather in existed for at least three hundred years after the death of Christ, so religious practices were vastly different from what our contemporary minds imagine. No attendance numbers are supplied because mere numerical growth was not the goal of the apostles, but rather authentic believers in Jesus Christ. Isn't it interesting that when they focused on making true believers, God added huge numbers of people? While we thankfully see conversions around us, for the last two decades the emphasis on "growth" has resulted in both fewer conversions *and* sagging attendance.

## CULTURAL DIFFERENCE

Many will argue that cultural differences make it harder for us to make true converts than it was for Paul. Centuries ago, they say, Paul didn't face the same opposition that we do. In these days of secular humanism, failing political leadership, and declining morality, Christian leaders claim we have more opposition to the spread of the gospel.

The truth is just the opposite.

Years one through one hundred of Christianity were the golden age of conversions. But those Christians had very little money and even less influence. The early church lived in a totally pagan culture. Degenerate emperors like Caligula and Nero were worshiped as gods and reigned over the world the apostles lived in as part of the Roman

Empire. On top of that, the emperors required taxes be paid to them. There was no prevailing sense of morality, as we call it. The emperors themselves were often immoral monsters who murdered their own family members. Belief in one God was ridiculed, and both Jews and Christians became easy targets for persecution.

We complain about the culture today, but despite their greater obstacles, we don't hear any complaints coming from the early Christians. *How are we going to build the church with Nero as the emperor? Come on. Let's be real. There's a totally pagan mentality over there in Rome.* Nobody was saying that. Instead, they just set about to obey the instructions of Jesus and trusted the Holy Spirit to overcome the challenges in front of them.

Why?

Because Jesus foretold it would be that way as they spread the gospel. They understood Jesus would build his church, his way, and for his glory. And they knew the Holy Spirit would empower, direct, and sustain them. And he did. People were converted, hundreds of churches were started, and the converts were truly born-again believers.

Obviously, a lot is wrong with our political leaders and the growing tide of ungodliness in our country. But our complaints don't match up with the reality of their more challenging circumstances. As Christians, we have had growing political involvement over the last forty years, but does anyone really believe that the Republicans, Democrats, White House, Supreme Court, or Congress will transform even one human heart? Are these civil servants supposed to be light and salt, or is that the task of the church of Jesus Christ?

Unless there is a new heart, there won't be a new person.

Unless people are changed, we can't have a transformed society, no matter who's in charge.

Moses gave Israel God's own holy law, and it didn't transform even one person on the inside. That's why God promised a new covenant and a better day when he said, "I will give you a new heart and put a new spirit in you; I will remove from you your heart of stone and give you a heart of flesh. And I will put my Spirit in you and move you to follow my decrees and be careful to keep my laws" (Ezek. 36:26–27). Whether for us as individuals, pastors, or church congregations, God's truth is the same: The gospel of Jesus alone changes people, and we must spread it everywhere. The new heart and new spirit he promised only happen when faith in Jesus Christ is preached.

It's a form of denial to say the reason we don't see the same results today is that we face greater opposition. Even more, our ability to spread the good news has been facilitated by technology and transportation, so we can communicate with people all over the world instantaneously.

No, the opposition hasn't changed; if anything has changed, it's been the message we are preaching.

## THE GOSPEL PREACHED IN AMERICA

That pure simple gospel of God's love and grace has been discarded or, in some cases, diluted by additives that are never mentioned in the New Testament. Consider these examples of the skewed gospels that people in America are now hearing.

*Join Our Church Gospel.* In this gospel, Christ is mentioned, but he shares the spotlight with the local church's name and image. When anything other than Christ is glorified, we aren't preaching the same gospel Peter and Paul shared. It's not at all about the Brooklyn Tabernacle; it's only and all about Jesus.

**The pure simple gospel of God's love and grace has been discarded or, in some cases, diluted by additives that are never mentioned in the New Testament.**

*Special Denomination Gospel.* This gospel starts with Jesus' message, but is layered with some supposed uniqueness of a man-made organization or denomination. Similarly, the *Calvinism Gospel* seems to aim more at proselytizing other Christians to a doctrinal position than seeing unbelievers come to faith in Christ. *Pentecostals* and *Charismatics* also can be guilty of emphasizing distinctive doctrinal positions more than Christ crucified. While doctrinal truth definitely has its place, that is not the simple gospel message they preached in Acts. Read the sermons of Peter and Paul, and you will notice that so many things we repeatedly hear today are *never* mentioned in their messages.

*Famous Pastor/Teacher Gospel.* Here the spotlight subtly shifts from Jesus alone to the supposed deep insights and dynamic skills of the speaker. But let's be real! God is not about to share any of the glory Jesus deserves with a Christian minister or teacher, no matter how gifted one is. The personalities of all our Christian leaders must fade into the background so Jesus can be on center stage by himself. As I read somewhere years ago, "You can't come across as clever and have Jesus wonderful at the same time." Every pastor ought to remember that as they start to speak.

*White American Cultural Gospel.* Here the message of Christ crucified is mixed with a lot of patriotic music, "stars and stripes," and "amber waves of grain." It's as if Jesus was born in Georgia! Its sister, the *Conservative Political Gospel,* is a development that has brought irreparable harm and confusion to those wanting to know who Jesus is. This message tries to enlist people into a cause, as if they were an army setting out to change society. Mean-spirited tirades against political enemies are a long way from the good news of Christ's sacrificial death for *all* of us on the cross.

The true gospel message isn't about laws or even morality; it is about the person of Jesus Christ. He alone forgives sin and transforms people into his likeness by his Spirit. Whenever we bring in our political positions, it grieves the Holy Spirit because from last I saw in the Bible, Jesus is neither a right-wing conservative nor a left-wing liberal. Some of those causes have validity, but a lot of them have an edge — sometimes a racial edge — or they're mixed with resentment against certain people groups. This is a far different spirit than that of heaven, where every nation, tribe, and color all worship as one before the Lord.

*Black or Latino Gospel.* Often as a backlash to the above, we find the mixing in of racial and ethnic themes that have nothing to do with salvation through Christ. I recently heard an African-American minister on the radio say, "The gospel of Jesus is about freedom." That certainly sounded biblical, but I was stunned when he further defined his terms. "God saved us to be free from the system!" It ended up being nothing more than black liberation theology — freedom from the oppression of the white man. While America has an exceedingly nasty history of race relations, this message will never give one person a new heart and pardon from sins.

These ramblings are not found in the gospel preaching of Peter and Paul. No one in the New Testament ever mentioned such things;

rather, they felt no race or ethnicity was worthy to be mentioned in the same sentence with Jesus Christ. "There is neither Jew nor Gentile, neither slave nor free, nor is there male and female, for you are all one in Christ Jesus" (Gal. 3:28). They didn't pit Jew against Gentile and Gentile against Jew. In fact they preached that we are all lost, we all need the same Savior, and we all need to love each other. And we can never improve on that message.

*Prosperity/Hyper-Faith Gospel.* This is an appealing but unbiblical message. It promises long life, health, and wealth to those who have "faith." But those who preach this gospel purposely ignore the Scriptures that tell us that when you accept Jesus, you could be martyred like some of the apostles. You could lose your friends and family, as Muslim converts do. Jesus said the world would hate us as they first hated him (John 15:18). Those who preach this prosperity gospel don't deliver the whole counsel of God but rather cherry-pick promises that appeal to people's natural appetites.

*Pietism with Prayer Gospel.* The teachers of this gospel confuse the message of salvation with the importance of spiritual growth. If you really love Jesus, they say, you need to prove it by being a prayer warrior of sorts, or accept other ascetic practices. You know what? As we have already seen with Hannah, the Bible has great promises concerning prayer, but that emphasis is not part of the gospel of Jesus. As important as it is, it's not the starting point for unbelievers. Repentance of sin and faith in Jesus is the only way to be born again.

*False Radicalism.* This is similar to the above misguided but well-intentioned consecration teaching — mixing discipleship with salvation. These teachers cite biblical stories, such as Jesus' encounter with the rich young ruler (Luke 18:18 – 30) who asked Jesus, "What must I do to inherit eternal life?"

Jesus said, "Obey the commandments."

"I've done that since I was a child," the rich young ruler replied.

Then Jesus looked at him and said, "Okay, one thing you lack. Go sell everything you have and give it to the poor and come follow me."

These preachers then turn to their audience and say, "Are you ready to give up everything to follow Jesus? If not, then you're not really a Christian."

Now, it's true you can take sentences out of the four Gospels that call for radical discipleship, but that's not the message of the gospel.

Jesus is never recorded as having told anyone else to sell everything he had. He only said that to the rich young ruler. And nowhere did Peter or Paul once include it as they proclaimed the good news of Jesus to Jew and Gentile alike. Instead, that work of consecration is something the Holy Spirit does *after* you are converted. It is not the gospel message! What has resulted is a "who's more radical" competition, which leads to pride and a looking away from Jesus.

*God Loves You with No Call to Repentance Gospel.* In this message, God's love is emphasized, but the call to repent and turn away from our sins is strangely absent. Ministers who preach this know that getting folks to confess they are sinners is a very difficult thing to do in the twenty-first century. That's why they just bypass it, saying, "Just receive Jesus." But that's not the full message of the gospel. There has to be a confession of sin first. You have to know you are sinking and lost before you can actually call on Christ as your Savior. Otherwise, why did he die? You can't change unless Christ changes you, but it must begin by turning *away* from sin and trusting Christ.

Let's not forget one of the more tragic developments among us. In reality, some of the *Church Growth Movement* seems almost anti-gospel. Their strategy is modeled after corporate America, and the stated goal is more about numerical growth than personal salvation through Christ. It is a mind set where numbers mean everything. Gradually, church growth "experts" have used attendance figures as an excuse or rationalization to slowly change the very meaning of Christianity. The New Testament gospel message is omitted or subtly altered to make sure folks come back the following week, often at the expense of preaching about sin, the cross of Christ, and personal salvation.

The strategy is "keep them coming back for more."

But for more of what?

Not once in the New Testament does Christ commission anyone to have a large church or ministry. He calls us to faithfully share the good news of salvation, in spite of the mixed reactions we know will come. The result of this embrace of worldly wisdom, which is "earthly" and "unspiritual" (James 3:15), has been truly catastrophic to the fiber of Christianity.

Many new paradigms of "church growth" have little resemblance

> **Christ calls us to faithfully share the good news of salvation, in spite of the mixed reactions we know will come.**

to New Testament spirituality and should be wept over rather than extolled. The leaders who advocate these approaches might sell books and become sought-after speakers, but ultimately no one can do anything against the truth. In their wake, these numerically minded leaders have brought about an increasing spiritual shallowness in the pew. In addition, they have pointed discouraged pastors to secular concepts rather than to the living Christ.

A recent ad for a church growth conference has a byline that says it all: "You'll hear the best ideas from the brightest minds...."

This says a lot about what the hook is for pastors searching for help. It's all about human cleverness and trendy ideas. The invitation listed some of the prominent names of those who would be speaking, but nowhere did it mention anything about God, prayer, or the power of the Holy Spirit.

## EVEN IN A "NEW DAY," IT'S AN OLD MESSAGE

We are living in an era when, for the first time in church history, spiritual leaders are being sold new methods instead of an opportunity to meet God in a fresh way. This philosophy has no historical precedent and, in reality, denies the person and work of the Holy Spirit.

Pastors tell me repeatedly that it's a "new day," and we must be careful not to offend or else folks might not visit again next Sunday. But when the message is catered to the people's tastes, soon it is no longer a message with God's power behind it. This is sad and has tragic consequences. We had better face the fact that Christ never asked us to be clever, entertaining communicators, but rather to declare his love and salvation to everyone we can.

Paul didn't end up in prison getting whipped and beaten, early Christians didn't face persecution, and Stephen didn't become martyred because they were broadcasting a "user-friendly" message. No, we are called by God to share the truth as it is in Jesus. We have to declare the pure, unadulterated gospel.

The Lord warned us that when we do it that way, in some situations, we will face the same hatred, the same rejection, and the same persecution that he faced. This is, of course, going on right now in the Middle East. Muslims are persecuting Christians in Egypt, and there have been dozens of church burnings. When Christians are discovered in Iran or in North Korea, terrible persecution occurs, including imprisonment and death. But the message won't change. It can't change. We must preach Christ and him crucified. Otherwise, we fail as followers of Jesus.

Now, that doesn't mean we should act in an unkind manner, so people are turned off because of our lack of politeness or grace. We *should* be concerned about relating to people — especially in relating to their spiritual condition and the battles they face daily. But we must preach the Word (2 Tim. 4:2)! No wonder many congregations are thinning out with some of the unbiblical and superficial drivel being spouted from the pulpit! The old saying, "You can't advertise a feast when there's no food on the table," is all too true, and we're seeing people vote with their feet as they drop out of the church scene.

When we tell people what they *need* to hear in a spirit of love, God will work in them, and many will trust in the Lord. If the gospel message is spoken with compassion and the help of the Spirit, lives will be touched and Jesus glorified. But it won't come by soft-selling the gospel or by mixing the message with other human ingredients.

Folks don't need God less today; that's impossible. But unless the speaker presents the truth boldly and lovingly, people will just sit week after week unchanged or find better things to do on a Sunday. We must preach the same Gospel that Peter and Paul did, and then we will see the kind of conversions they experienced.

## PAUL'S MESSAGE IN THESSALONICA

In his letter to the Thessalonians, Paul reminds them that the gospel was what he preached to them. He calls it specifically "our gospel" because, like today, a number of counterfeit gospels were being preached. Paul's gospel was the message he had received directly from the Lord Jesus himself and not taught to him by any religious school or council of men. It was the good news about Christ.

The secret to Paul's success is obvious, and he openly shares it. "For I am not ashamed of the gospel, because it is the power of God that brings salvation to everyone who believes: first to the Jew, then to the Gentile" (Rom. 1:16). That powerful gospel of Jesus produced results back then, and it has not lost its power over the centuries. The gospel is the power of God bringing salvation to sinners. Nothing else in this world, or in the Bible, expresses God's love like the good news of Jesus Christ dying for our sins.

Accepting that truth, we are forced to only one conclusion. We ministers and our churches apparently are not proclaiming the same gospel that Paul did. How else can we explain the difference in spiritual results?

**Paul's gospel message was full of the supernatural ... and that supernatural gospel bore supernatural results.**

The gospel message has not lost its power.

Unfortunately, as I wrote above, we have altered the message, adding things that aren't there and taking away things that are.

If you read carefully all the gospel sermons recorded in the book of Acts (e.g., Acts 2, 3, 10, 13, 20, 22), you will notice that the gospel came with a simple purity. It spoke of God's love, humankind's sinful, lost condition, and the remedy provided only through Jesus Christ — the shedding of his blood on the cross and subsequent resurrection. It asked for repentance from sin and childlike faith in Christ.

Nothing more.

That was the secret of the power of the gospel as huge numbers of people turned away from their old lives and became new creations in Christ. They were, as Jesus called it, born again (John 3)! Paul's gospel message was full of the supernatural — a virgin birth, God in the form of man bearing the world's sins on his body, a resurrection from the dead — and that supernatural gospel bore supernatural results.

## WE SHARE THE MESSAGE, GOD SAVES

Even so, Paul's message was rejected as often as it was accepted, and it was usually the cross that was the stumbling block for the ancient unbelievers, much as it still is today.

Greek culture loved beauty, and the idea of a crucified God was ridiculous to them. "For the message of the cross is foolishness to those who are perishing, but to us who are being saved it is the power of God" (1 Cor. 1:18). They didn't want to hear about a carpenter's son who was massacred: stripped until he was almost naked, beaten to a pulp, and then dying on a cross. They had no desire to worship something they saw as so ugly.

The Romans believed in power and exercised it everywhere they went. The idea of God's Son being identified as a criminal, a loser, and a victim on a cross was impossible for them to even consider. They glorified strength, and the Roman Empire was built on the philosophy that might makes right.

The Jews knew from their scriptures that everyone who hung on a tree was cursed (Deut. 21:22 – 23). What a stumbling block for them to become believers! How could their Messiah die on a cross?

Paul faced these challenges and more, yet he still preached the cross of Christ unflinchingly.

We see similar stumbling blocks in our churches today. The gospel of Jesus crucified for the sins of the world is a hindrance to many because it describes all of us as sinners needing a Savior. Proud men and women of the twenty-first century recoil at such a humbling indictment against them.

In addition, the gospel often invokes harsh reactions against the minister or believer in Christ who shares it. "Who are you to judge?" is the reply we often hear. But God himself is the one who has judged all of us as sinners, needing the remedy he lovingly provided in his only Son — Jesus.

To others, the whole idea of God, sin, and salvation is dismissed out of hand as an outdated, primitive superstition.

No matter. Our personal task is not to save souls, but to faithfully share the gospel of Jesus and the cross, which is the power that will accomplish all.

Not everyone will believe. In fact, this is why Jesus ended up on a cross and Christian ministers and believers were often hounded out of town or suffered abuse and persecution. But these are the facts of spiritual life on planet earth, and we must not shrink from the commission our Lord gave us to spread his message to everyone we can.

## IT'S ALL ABOUT JESUS AND HIS SACRIFICE FOR OUR SINS

Some years ago I made my own careful study of gospel preaching in the New Testament. I was convicted and humbled. As a result, I wanted to destroy many of my past sermons. Many of my early sermons were a "Moses/Jesus" gospel — mixing legalism from the Old Testament with the grace of the New Testament centered in Jesus.

This is still a prevalent practice today among preachers and teachers. It is fine to preach a sermon from the Old Testament, but you can't end there. The apostles used references from the Old Testament for one reason: to point to Jesus Christ and the salvation he alone offers.

Some prominent preachers have admitted privately to me that they also, at times, have preached sermons from Old Testament themes without ever getting back to Jesus, the cross, the Holy Spirit, and the new life promised us in the gospel. Our subject matter should always be the same as that of the apostles who were told by an angel to go "and tell the people all about *this new life*" (Acts 5:20).

What new life?

The new spiritual life we can have only through Christ, "who is your life" (Col. 3:4).

God once spoke through Samuel, but that is not our message. We must remember that "In the past God spoke to our ancestors through the prophets at many times and in various ways, but in these last days he has spoken to us by his Son" (Heb. 1:1 – 2).

God has given us many truths in the Bible, but his final word to all of us is Jesus! Every answer to every problem is found in Jesus. The only true image of the invisible God is Jesus.

The greatest of all the apostles confirms this all-encompassing subject when he says, "But we preach *Christ* crucified: a stumbling block to Jews and foolishness to Gentiles, but to those whom God has called, both Jews and Greeks, *Christ the power of God* and the *wisdom of God* (1 Cor. 1:23 – 24). And again, "For I resolved to know *nothing* while I was with you except Jesus Christ and him crucified" (1 Cor. 2:2). The word on every pastor's and believer's lips should be "Jesus," for only in him is there pardon, power, wisdom, and the new beginning people are longing for. It's totally irrelevant what spiritual forces or human hardness confront us, because the gospel of Jesus is still "the power of God" to save and transform people in our own personal mission field.

So what does it all mean?

By shunning or diluting the gospel message, we have ended up with less influence on unbelievers and decreasing spirituality among professing believers. All the statistics irrefutably confirm this. No one who loves Jesus can be happy with the current state of affairs. But it can dramatically change if we return to the message God gave us to share with our friends, community, and world.

Let's study afresh what the gospel message means, even if we have been believers for decades. Let's ask the Holy Spirit for boldness to speak it in love no matter the reactions toward us. Let's pray for pastors and for ourselves that we become lighthouses in an increasingly dark world as we "hold firmly to the word of life" in Jesus (Phil. 2:16).

> **The current state of affairs can dramatically change if we return to the message God gave us to share with our friends, community, and world.**

This is beautifully illustrated in the fruitful ministry of the evangelist Billy Graham. He traveled around the world for decades, humbly and faithfully declaring one simple message — the gospel of Jesus Christ. No matter what country he was in, or what his audience might want to hear, Billy Graham was going to preach Jesus and his death on the cross and resurrection.

I still remember seeing him on a top-rated late night talk show decades ago. He was barely greeted before he found an opening to declare, "For God so loved the world that he gave his one and only Son, that whoever believes in him shall not perish but have eternal life" (John 3:16).

It seemed if you squeezed Billy Graham, the gospel of Christ would flow out from him! He might not have been the slickest preacher around, but look at the countless souls saved by this simple message from a simple man. Like the apostle Paul, he was always preaching "Jesus Christ and him crucified."

Nothing more. Nothing less.

And this must be our only message too.

# Chapter 9

# A SONG IN THE DARK

Karen's Story

*Karen Rampersad is one of the most talented soloists the Brooklyn Tabernacle Choir has ever had. She has sung around the world with the choir and has performed solos on many of the choir's CDs. Whether on the streets of a third-world country, at a prominent church in the United States, or in a concert hall in Japan, Karen's pure voice lights up the darkness with a song.*

*This is a pretty remarkable feat, considering that Karen was first dedicated not to God, but to Satan.*

*Her parents, originally from Honduras, were introduced to Santeria — a satanic Latino religion that perverts elements of Catholicism. Growing up, Karen attended religious ceremonies where she witnessed people being possessed by evil spirits, and she feared those spirits would do the same to her.*

*Though Karen and her parents were blind to the powers of darkness that gripped them at the time, through the intercessory prayers of her sister, Karen was eventually led out of darkness and introduced to the good news of Jesus Christ. Now Karen uses her voice to reach into the darkest corners of our world and bring the good news of Jesus to those who are as confused as she once was.*

## KAREN

I grew up in Coney Island in a neighborhood that wasn't very safe. While it wasn't as crazy an area as the Bronx or East New York, neither was it a resort town. I was the second of three daughters born to first-generation immigrants from Honduras. Everything about Coney Island was foreign to my parents. In Honduras they had lived in a rural setting; now they were living in Brooklyn, one of the five boroughs of New York City — one of the largest urban areas in America. Everything was new to them, including the language and local customs. Despite the challenges facing them, they were good parents, strict and attentive, but I felt they were overly *protective*.

Growing up, I had a Puerto Rican godmother whom I called Madrina — which is Spanish for "godmother." She was older than my parents and in many ways helped them navigate their new country. Madrina was also our spiritual guide, and we looked to her for religious advice. Though we grew up Catholic, we deviated from the standard practices. Different words described what we did. Some called it voodoo, black magic, white magic, or Santeria. Some tried it to get blessings, while others cursed people with it. We never cursed anyone, stuck pins in dolls, or wished anyone harm, but neither did we know what harm it could cause us.

When I was about eight or nine, my godmother supposedly saw a gift in me. Madrina told my mother that I would be able to see people's futures and that I had the gift of palm reading. On her word, it was decided that I would be dedicated or set apart. But no one asked who or what I was being dedicated to, and I was too young to think much about it. On the day of the dedication, I remember being told to wear yellow because we were going to Madrina's house. We often went to my godmother's house for meals and to talk or just to hang out.

But this night was different.

When we arrived, Madrina took us to her basement where her altar was located. Candles lit the room; it smelled of candles, incense, and herbs. My family watched as my godmother led me to the front of the room. There she prayed some kind of blessing over me, and then took a coconut, cracked it, and poured the coconut water over my head. I knew I was being dedicated, but I didn't really understand what that meant.

My parents didn't see any harm in what they were doing. In fact, they thought they were harnessing the good power that Madrina had recognized in me. They believed that the ritual set me apart and made me special.

I didn't feel special. I just felt wet.

When we returned home, Madrina instructed my parents to create an altar in my room. The altar was a bureau of sorts, and on it we placed several statues my godmother helped them acquire. There was one of Lazarus (the beggar in one of Jesus' parables) on crutches with dogs licking his wounds, and another was of the archangel Michael. There were also several of the Virgin Mary, including a statue of the Caridad Del Cobre, the patron saint of Cuba, and one with Mary stepping on a snake. But the one I remember the most was a colorful statue of an oversized hand with a bloody scar in the palm. A different saint adorned the tip of each finger.

Some might have found this disturbing, but I didn't.

From the fifth through the eighth grades, I attended a Catholic school, and we would pray to the statues and kiss the crucifix at school or at mass, so it didn't seem odd that I would do the same at home. Madrina gave me a book of prayers to recite, and many of them were the same ones I prayed at church. I would kneel in front of the altar in my room, praying to the statues in front of me, repeating the Hail Mary and the Our Father, along with other prayers to St. Lazarus and my guardian angel. We were told to burn incense and candles. Madrina instructed me on how to leave offerings of fruit, cake, and candy on the altar. Again, this didn't seem odd to me. I learned that on certain holidays in Honduras, members of my extended family would always fill an extra plate and leave the food offerings in the corner with a glass of water for the ancestral spirits.

Though my younger sister shared my room with me, I was the only one of us three girls who had an altar or knelt in front of it to say prayers. I was under the impression that God was a judge, and if I didn't say my prayers exactly as I had been taught, God wouldn't like me and I would go straight to hell. In my mind, the Catholicism of school and the Santeria of my godmother all seemed the same. If there were differences, I didn't notice. I never questioned what I was asked to do or why my sisters didn't have to do it. I was an easygoing child. I just did as I was told — except when it came to singing.

I loved to sing. I sang just because I liked hearing myself sing.

But no one in my family enjoyed my voice as much as I did. My singing annoyed my parents. "Keep it down!" they'd yell at me. Doors slammed when I lifted my voice in song, but I couldn't help it; I loved music. Unfortunately, the only music we were allowed to have in the house was the radio and occasionally (when they let us watch it) the TV. When they were on, I would sing along no matter whom it disturbed.

> **I was under the impression that God was a judge, and if I didn't say my prayers exactly as I had been taught, God wouldn't like me and I would go straight to hell.**
>
> —*Karen*

While my parents were protecting me from bad outside influences, members of my extended family were exposing me to dangerous things — things I shouldn't have been exposed to. I had my first drink when I was nine. We were at a family party, and someone thought it would be cute to offer me wine, so some man handed me a cup and said, "Here, drink this." I thought it tasted funny, but I drank it all. From then on, I continued to drink at family events when I could get away with it. This experience and others led me to believe that adults, especially men, were untrustworthy, and I would have to learn to take care of myself.

Madrina continued to be a huge influence on my family and me. We often went to her house for gatherings, and she would come to ours. But one night those innocent get-togethers took an evil turn.

I was in fifth grade, and we had gathered with about forty people in my godmother's basement, where her altar was located. My altar was nothing compared to hers. She had more statues than I did, and they were bigger and more colorful. Huge shrines and collections of oversized figurines spilled out from one corner of the room. The place was aglow with dozens of flickering candles. Fragrant incense burned, giving the place a hazy, smoky feeling.

Looking around the room, I could see Puerto Ricans and Dominicans. As Hondurans, we were the only black Latino family, and we were the only children there. I sat next to my mother and watched men and women with colorful scarves praying and chanting in Spanish as they made drink offerings to the statues. I was told they were chanting, "Blessed be the name of the lord." That sounded like a nice thing to say, but I could tell from the horrible dark expressions on their faces that there was nothing joyous about their blessing.

People began walking around the room or kneeling and praying. Some were speaking gibberish in foreign-sounding tongues. They were not acting like themselves. I watched as a spirit overtook Madrina. First her eyes glazed over, and her whole countenance changed. Then she started speaking in a strange and different voice. People would walk up to her, and she would tell them they needed to change something in their life or that something bad would happen to them. To some, she appeared angry.

"Do you have anything to say to me?" they would each ask the spirit she was channeling.

Though I couldn't hear what she said, I could tell she was reprimanding them. She would put her hands on their shoulders and push them away. Through it all, her eyes had a steady, uncomfortable gaze, and she never smiled.

Someone or something possessed her, that was for sure!

Mother decided I needed to talk to the spirit. She took me by the hand, and we stood in line until it was our turn to approach Madrina. When we walked up to her, without warning, Madrina reached out and grabbed each of my ears and pulled as if she was trying to tear them off my head. I did my best not to cry out, and eventually she stopped. If she said anything to us, I didn't hear it, because I was too stunned by what had just happened.

As we made our way back to our seats on the sofa, I asked my mother, "Why did she do that?"

"I don't know, but I am guessing it's because you're a stubborn girl and you don't listen. That's why. You should listen to your parents."

I rubbed my ears and thought that made sense. I knew there were times I didn't listen.

Looking around the room, I could see others who also were staring vacantly as if in a trance or some hypnotic state. I watched as a spirit overtook a man who stood in the middle of the room and was drinking from a glass. His eyes suddenly turned blank and cold, and his face became distorted and angry. A chill ran down my spine because he was so dark and scary looking.

People rushed to help him sit in a chair. His voice altered drastically, and he cried out. Then without warning, the man passed out. When he lost consciousness, the glass dropped, red juice spilled, and pieces of glass flew everywhere. When he hit the floor, his chair turned over, and more people rushed to his aid.

It was the scariest thing I had ever seen, and I was frightened out of my mind. I practically jumped on top of my mother, drawing her arm around me until I buried my head in her armpit, like a chick hiding under its mother's wing.

I could hear people saying, "Praise the lord!" in Spanish.

From somewhere deep inside me, I felt something say, "That's not God." It was a fleeting voice that was there and gone.

I heard a commotion and finally dared to peek out from my mother's protective cover. I watched as they carried the man to the courtyard and laid him out back. I felt a presence in the room, and all I could think was, *Please don't come for me!*

For the rest of the evening, I was paralyzed by fear while ritualistic sacrifices and prayers continued to the chants of "Praise the lord." What lord was this they were talking about? Whoever they were talking to was the opposite of the Lord that I thought I knew. Their god was scary!

As the evening continued, I was overwhelmed with fear and couldn't wait to get out of there. On the way home that night, I remember thinking, *That can't be God, and if it is God, then I want nothing to do with him!* Something happened inside of me on our trip back home — I closed my mind and my heart to what I saw going on around me. I decided that if this is what God offered, I wanted nothing to do with him. He was scary and evil, and I didn't want any part of what he was offering.

Over the next year, things started to change. Perhaps my parents were spooked by what they saw that night because we saw less of Madrina. Without her presence in the family, I didn't feel the need to pray at the altar as much as I once had.

Eventually she stopped coming over at all, and I stopped praying. Without a spiritual mentor, we eventually dismantled the altar and moved the statues to a closet. Other than those changes, our family life continued much as it had before. We went to mass every Sunday, and my parents continued to be strict and protective, not allowing me out of the house much. But my need for freedom and independence increased. I would beg them to let me go places, and when they said no, I'd whine and complain. They could see I was becoming more rebellious, and I think they made an extra effort to keep an eye on me.

When I was thirteen, my older sister, Delmis, entered high school, and a friend invited her to go to church at the Brooklyn Tabernacle.

The very first time Delmis attended services, she gave her heart to the Lord and came to know Jesus Christ as her personal Lord and Savior.

Then the next thing she did was go into battle for my soul. She started fighting for me in prayer. I wanted nothing to do with God, religion, church, or any of it. Over the years, I had come to the conclusion that it was too much work to be in a right standing with God. I had spent years trying to earn my way to heaven by saying all of those prayers. Now I was over and done with it. I didn't know exactly what it took to get to heaven, but I would figure it out. All I really wanted to do was hang out with my girlfriends, and I started developing an interest in boys.

> **I had conflicting views on God, and while I began to realize he might not be as scary as I once thought, I wasn't sure he had anything to offer me.**
>
> —*Karen*

I had conflicting views on God, and while I began to realize he might not be as scary as I once thought, I wasn't sure he had anything to offer me. As I watched Delmis pray and read her Bible, I assumed God just wanted to add to my to-do list. But I was done with all of that.

Every week, Delmis would beg me to go to church with her. I had found mass boring, and I couldn't see how Delmis's new church would be any different. Besides, it was nearly an hour commute to the church. Why would I want to go there, when I could go to mass just a few blocks away? Whenever she asked, I'd just say, "No, thank you."

But Delmis wouldn't give up. Each week she persisted, begging me to come at least once with her to church or youth group. She even enlisted her friends to pray for me. On several occasions I would meet someone for the first time, and they would tell me they already knew me because they had been praying for me.

I remember one person saying, "Every time they ask for prayer requests, Delmis speaks up and says, 'Pray for my sister Karen.'"

I didn't know it at the time, but I needed those prayers. At home, I felt as if my parents had a death grip on my life. Whenever I got a little freedom, I would go crazy. I was on my way to being a party girl. I started messing around with boys, but fortunately, before I could round the bases, something inside would always stop me. "No, I don't want to do that right now," I'd tell the guy I was with, confusing him with my fickleness. Other times, the guy would stop *me*! Looking back, I believe Delmis's prayers prevented me from going further.

Still thirteen, I finally gave in and went to church with Delmis for the first time, just to shut her up. During that service, Pastor Cymbala talked about how much Jesus loved us. My heart was touched. While it was an emotional moment, I didn't let it affect my decision making. My heart was too hardened. I was more worried about the fact that the service ran more than two hours! Plus, from our home in Coney Island to Brooklyn Tabernacle, it was a forty-five minute commute each way. Why would I want to spend four hours doing what I could do at Catholic mass in about an hour?

But I did sense the joy that was in the church as they worshiped, and I loved the choir. Delmis would bring home Brooklyn Tabernacle Choir albums and play them at home. I always sang along, not thinking about what the lyrics meant, even after I knew them all by heart.

Delmis continued to pray for me and invite me to church, youth group, or other special events at Brooklyn Tabernacle. Occasionally she would wear me down (or I needed a reason to get out of the house), and I would join her. Once I remember her pulling me by my scarf, as she literally dragged me to the church. That girl didn't give up easily!

I felt a joy and peace when I was at the church, and there were some aspects I really liked. I specifically remember attending a Brooklyn Tabernacle Choir concert at Radio City Music Hall. By then, I had been singing along with the albums for some time, and I knew all the words to every song. The hall was so beautiful, and the choir was so famous, it was like watching my favorite celebrities perform in concert. These people all looked perfect and like they didn't have a care in the world. They knew exactly who they were and what they were supposed to do.

I didn't have a clue what I was supposed to do.

When I entered high school, I had no goals in life, no aim, no nothing. With no plans and protective parents, I was home a lot. So on those rare occasions I got to attend a party, I drank, and it loosened me up so I could have a good time. I loved to be around people, to dance and get loud. At parties, I'd mess around with guys, but again, something would stop me before I could go all the way.

In April 1990, the week before I turned seventeen, my cousin and I planned to go to a party being held the same weekend as the Brooklyn Tabernacle youth retreat. Delmis had some money and was going to the retreat. She asked if I wanted to come too. I had been to the church enough that I had made some friends, but the pull of a retreat in Pennsylvania didn't compare to the pull of a weekend party — especially since I'd already gotten permission from my strict parents to go.

No matter how much Delmis wanted me to go with her, I knew this retreat was one event even she couldn't drag me to because my family couldn't afford the $85 to send me.

But Delmis didn't give up easily. She started praying. Out of nowhere, my mother changed her mind and revoked her permission for me to attend the party. "If you don't go to this retreat, you're not going anywhere this weekend!" she said.

I couldn't believe it! *What made her change her mind?* I resigned myself spending another weekend at home. But something truly unexpected happened. I came home from school one day, and my sisters were dancing and shouting. "Papi won a thousand dollars!"

Papi had been playing the numbers, and he won the lottery. There was more than enough money to pay the bills, buy food for the family, and pay for me to go to the retreat. There was no question now — I was going, and the whole family was celebrating.

"Oh, that's good!" I said. Truthfully, I wasn't happy about the sudden change of events. I didn't expect much to happen at the retreat, but I had a few friends who would be there, and I decided I would just make the best of it. At least I wouldn't have to stay home.

Yet something happened inside of me that Saturday night as I listened to a woman give her testimony. Though she was married to a pastor, she talked about how she had failed terribly and then came back to Christ.

*Hmm! Maybe I don't have to be perfect,* I thought for the first time.

Inside of my mind, I started to feel as if a fight was taking place. Though I was sitting and listening to her just like everyone else in the room, something inexplicable was happening inside of me. Jesus was calling to me and asking me to do something I didn't want to do. Though it wasn't audible, I felt like he was saying to me, "Give me your heart."

As the evening continued, the program finished, and the others got up to leave the large room where we had assembled. But I didn't move. I sat in the same spot not moving, with a battle raging inside of me as I argued with God.

"Come to me." He was sweet and gentle, but I refused to give in.

*No, I don't want to give my life to you. I don't need any more regulations and rules to follow, I've had enough.*

"Please come to me."

*I've said all the prayers a person can say over the years, I'm exhausted, I'll just do it myself.*

"I'll help you, if you only come to me."

He wouldn't give up on me. Though I was independent and wanted to remain that way, I could feel myself growing weaker and finding fewer arguments for why I shouldn't give in. At the same time, I knew that saying no to God was saying yes to an aimless life.

Finally, I couldn't fight it any longer. I accepted the fact that without the Lord, my life would be empty and aimless. I knew I needed Jesus Christ because I was a loose cannon and life on my own wouldn't be good.

*Okay, Lord. You win. Have it your way. Whatever it is you want me to do, I'll do it. I have no clue what it is, but I'm tired of fighting.*

Suddenly, I was overwhelmed with feelings of peace and joy. I started to cry the way I'd cried that day in church, but this was different—the tears wouldn't stop. I told my friends there what happened, but the next day when the leader asked if anyone wanted to accept Jesus Christ as Savior, I still raised my hand as a public sign.

I knew the change was real because in the days and weeks that followed, I suddenly had a desire to read my Bible and attend church. A few weeks later, I was baptized, and within a few months I was singing with the Brooklyn Tabernacle Youth Chorale. It was there that I discovered I had a gift, and it had nothing to do with telling the future. It had everything to do with God's plan for my future.

I had a gift of music I had never recognized before, but others, especially at Brooklyn Tab, noticed. One day a friend of mine said to the choir leader, "I think you should give Karen a solo."

I had never sung a solo before, and I had no idea why she said that.

The choir leader must have been equally surprised. "Karen, who is always fooling around? That Karen?"

> Finally, I couldn't fight it any longer. I accepted the fact that without the Lord, my life would be empty and aimless.
>
> —Karen

"Yes," my friend responded. "I've heard her sing, and you should consider giving her a solo."

The next thing I knew, I was asked to sing a solo with the choir.

At the time, the church was located on Flatbush Avenue, and the sanctuary seated more than a thousand people. As I got up to sing a solo with the youth choir, I knew it was a big deal. It was the first time I ever sang in front of anyone other than my family — and we know how well *that* had gone. I was so nervous that throughout the song I could feel myself shaking. I was afraid I'd look like the fool everyone thought I was.

When I finished, I was relieved to see smiles of appreciation and hear the audience applaud.

Pastor Cymbala stood up to take the offering and said, "I want that young lady to come back and sing again." He wanted the choir to repeat the song and wanted me to sing the solo *again*! I hadn't even stopped shaking from the first time.

Pastor Cymbala's wife, Carol, wasn't in the sanctuary, so he sent someone to get her. As the founder and director of the Brooklyn Tabernacle Choir, she needed to hear me, he thought. As we sang, he felt he heard God whisper to him, "Help her. You need to help her. Take her under your wing." They soon invited me to stay over at their home and took a loving interest in my life, which continues to this day. Of course, I didn't know any of that was going on. I was too busy singing and trembling in my shoes!

Soon I was a regular soloist in the youth choir and then about a year later, with the main choir. I was only nineteen years old when I started soloing with the Brooklyn Tabernacle Choir — the same choir I'd watched at Radio City Music Hall and whose albums I used to sing along with.

Since then, I have traveled a lot with the choir and have sung many album solos. God obviously had a plan for my life, and it meant protecting me from the satanic atmosphere I was introduced into as a child. When I started following Jesus, not only did I discover my gift, but I also discovered my future.

Despite my early interest in boys, I remained single until I was thirty-nine. (Fortunately, I didn't know that when I was sixteen!) Though I prayed and prayed for a husband, it didn't happen until one day when I met a man from Trinidad at the church and we started talking.

After we had been friends for a few months, we were having a quiet conversation about his homeland. "I was in Trinidad once," I said.

I explained that it was the first overseas trip I took with Pastor Cymbala and friends from the choir. I told him how I fell in love with the culture when I made some friends from Trinidad at church, and how I had been praying for a Trinidadian husband ever since. "As part of the evangelistic outreach, we had a concert in Port of Spain, the capital of Trinidad — it was in Woodford Square. Do you know where that is?" I asked.

"I was there," he said.

"No, you weren't."

"Sweetie, I was there. I walked by and saw the sign; it said 'Brooklyn Tabernacle.' I saw this guy on the stage singing, 'I Can Be Glad.'"

"Please don't tell me that! I was standing right behind him singing backup!"

We both marveled at how our paths had crossed, but God did not allow us to actually meet until eighteen years later!

As I tell this story, it is exactly three years from the day I met Tyron. We were married two months ago, and I continue to solo with the choir. My mother rededicated her heart to the Lord years ago, and Papi gave his heart to the Lord years later.

Looking over my life, I can see it has been anything but boring! Madrina may have sensed something special about me, and she certainly had plans for me, but God's mercy said, "No!" He gave me a gift, and he wanted it used to glorify him. Now my life has a purpose and my music has meaning. While I thank God for that, I also thank my sister. If Delmis had not persistently prayed for me, I don't know where I would be. Despite all of my parents' efforts to protect me, I think Jesus used Delmis's prayers to protect me from myself, from enemies in the unseen world, and eventually to soften my heart so I could hear his voice calling me into a relationship with him.

# Chapter 10

# STORM TEAM

The Power of Intercessory Prayer

I have been a shepherd, and I have been one of the sheep. But one of the times I felt the most unity and brotherhood was when I played as a Ram.

Back in my college days, I played basketball for the University of Rhode Island (URI). Each year as a URI Ram basketball player, nothing was more exciting than the thought of an invitation to the NCAA Tournament that took place every year in March. Today, sixty-four teams are invited to play in the tournament, but back then there were only twenty-two. To be eligible for the tournament, your team had to either win your league or receive a bid from the tournament committee. Out of the thousands of colleges and universities in the United States, only the best would play in the elimination tournament.

Our team wanted to win our conference and make "the big dance."

In my senior year of college, I was captain of the team and played point guard. By the close of the season, we had a great record and were in first place for our division. We were one game ahead of our rival, the University of Connecticut, and we had one game left in the regular season.

Unfortunately, our last game was against UConn. At UConn.

If we won, we would win the Yankee Conference title and automatically enter the tournament.

But if we lost, we would have to play a tiebreaker.

UConn had, and still has, a strong home court advantage, and they used it that night. Thousands of people showed up for the game, screaming and cheering for the home team. Toward the close of the game, UConn was blowing us out, but we kept fighting. Tensions escalated on both sides of the court when suddenly one of the UConn players punched our center, opening a cut above his eye. The referee missed the initial punch, but turned around in time to see my teammate Art swinging a punch in retaliation. The referee whistled, stopped the play, and threw Art out of the game. That infuriated our team.

When my friend left the court, the referee saw blood flowing from the cut above his eye, and he clearly realized he had missed something — but it was too late. We had to finish the game without Art, but it really didn't matter. We got a beatdown from an excellent UConn team.

That meant we were forced to play a tiebreaker. The winner would go on to the NCAA Tournament, and the loser would go home. Since our records were tied, conference officials had to flip a coin to see where the playoff game would be held — and who had the home court advantage.

A few nights later, we were once again on our way back to Storrs, Connecticut — UConn had won the toss. Because of how the last game ended, the guys on the bus were bitter. The whole team knew the game would be televised from Maine to Connecticut. All of the New England coast would be watching, including our family and friends at URI. We knew how much was at stake, and we were wound so tight that you could bounce the tension in the bus like a basketball. If we won, we'd be in the tournament; if we lost, well . . . it would be a long, depressing bus ride home.

Despite the looming battle we faced on the court, on the bus we were united and determined to play together as a team. Throughout the bus you could hear echoes of "Play as a team!" and "Stand together as a team." Individual players promised each other, "Don't worry, I got your back." And we meant it as we huddled before the opening tipoff: "No matter what, we're a team."

When you play together as a team, you play winning basketball.

That night the URI Rams played as a team.

We were cohesive with no individual egos getting in the way. We knew that as a band of brothers, we could overcome anything that UConn threw at us on the court, including their fists. Win or lose, that night we would play for each other and not for ourselves.

**We often forget that serving Christ is a team sport. If we want to win against the powers of darkness in this world, we have to be united and work together.**

Have you ever felt that kind of unity and brotherhood?

Have you ever experienced it in your church?

Do your brothers and sisters in your church have *your* back?

I think we often forget that serving Christ is a team sport. If we want to win against the powers of darkness in this world, we have to be united and work together.

## STORM TEAMS

When an especially bad storm is expected to hit, news stations in major cities often bring out their "Storm Team." Typically, what this means is that two or more meteorologists will be working together to keep viewers informed on watches and warnings for the area. It may also mean that reporters are pulled off their usual beats to cover the storm effects — especially if damage is expected. When a hurricane is scheduled to hit Florida, you will often see several people working together to board up windows. When floods hit the Midwest, entire communities turn out to fill sandbags. These individuals can't stop a storm, but working together, they can minimize the damaging effects.

So why don't we work together when storms hit the church?

When a storm hits the church, it affects all of us. More than ever, we need to unite under the banner of Christ. If one member of the body is experiencing spiritual warfare, we all should be sensitive to it. If one part of the body is in pain, the whole body is in pain. Yet it seems that when the church is in crisis, we are more likely to fight against *each other* than we are to fight together against the *effects of the storm*. When things start declining, individuals blame the pastor, small churches blame megachurches, and certain denominations tend to criticize other denominations.

Why do we do this when together we can do something about it?

As captain of the basketball team, I said to my teammates, "We're a team. We can't be prima donnas. We play together. We fight together. We lose together. We win together." As the pastor of Brooklyn Tabernacle, I am still saying those same things, only now I apply them to my congregation.

One of the greatest weapons God has given us is the ability to fight together, locking arms in intercessory prayer and saying, "You are not going to quit and go down. I'm not just praying for myself; I'm looking out for you!"

A pastor's job is to preach to and teach their congregation. The good ones love their people, and the best ones hang out with them socially. But they also have to teach their people to unite together in *prayer for each other*.

One reason I believe pastors don't teach much on this subject is that we don't practice it ourselves. One of the greatest failings of pastors, starting with me, is that we don't pray enough for our people. Like everyone else, we can be caught up in our own family issues and our own problems. But as pastors, we must pray for our church members and encourage them to do the same.

Intercessory prayer is rarely emphasized in many churches, but it is a powerful weapon given to us by Christ for spiritual warfare. Have we ever needed it more than right now while we are in the midst of a storm?

We should all link arms with others in the body of Christ and pray for each other at every opportunity. If we want to turn back the tide that threatens to overwhelm the church, there is no better way than through intercessory prayer.

## PAUL PRAYS FOR HIS PEOPLE

In an earlier chapter, Bethsaida mentioned how, at one time in her life, her prayers were very me-centered. She isn't the only one who deals with that. Most of us pray mainly for ourselves. *Bless me; help me; I need a job; I need healing; help me get that raise; I need a new car. God, you know how lonely I feel; please send me a companion.* When we're done talking about us, we are usually done praying.

But this wasn't true in the days of the New Testament church. The apostle Paul writes about how he constantly prayed for the Christians to whom he ministered. In Ephesians, he says, "For this reason I kneel before the Father," and "I pray that out of his glorious riches he may strengthen *you* with power through his Spirit in *your* inner being" (Eph. 3:14, 16).

We can learn two things from Paul in this passage. First, he must have thought that prayer is powerful. Why would he waste his time praying if he didn't think God would respond? Paul loved his people so much that he got down on his knees and prayed for them, knowing there are certain things that God only does in answer to prayer. Prayer was the result of Paul's love for his people, but the *reason* he prayed is that he knew it was effective. The simple teaching of Scripture is that God accomplishes great things in response to prayer. Martin Luther said that God does almost nothing except in answer to prayer. So if we neglect praying for one another, we will forfeit the blessings God has waiting for his people.

But there is a second truth in this passage. Paul knew that through prayer, God would strengthen the people with power from the Spirit. Pastors who are mostly concerned about preaching sermons might say to Paul, "Why don't you just *teach* them power?"

That's the point! Christianity is not primarily a teaching religion. Teaching is involved; in fact, I'm trying to do that now as I write these words. But Christianity isn't like Mormonism, Jehovah's Witness, or Islam. Those are teaching religions. In those religions and others, leaders instruct followers until they reach a certain level of knowledge, and then their members are often inducted into an inner circle based on what they have learned.

Christianity, on the other hand, is essentially a supernatural religion. Jesus is God in the flesh. He was born of a virgin. He bore the sins of the world on himself as he died. He rose from the dead. He promises the gift of eternal life to those who receive him.

Heaven is promised *to us.*

The Holy Spirit lives *within us.*

These are all supernatural facts. They are the foundation of Christianity. But individual and corporate prayer no longer flourish, mainly because the church has lost faith in the supernatural God. We no longer believe in a God who answers in supernatural ways. When that kind of unbelief prevails, prayer dies.

Because of the prevailing anti-supernatural teaching in the Christian church over the last few decades, the Holy Spirit has been politely asked to leave the premises. This has taken away from God's original plan for his church and left us as merely lecture halls where sound doctrine is being regularly expounded. But that is not the religion of Jesus as modeled in the New Testament. Ministers are supposed to lead their congregations into fellowship with God himself and not merely their slant on truth with innovative props and illustrations.

Is this about experiencing Jesus in a fresh way or merely hearing a great sermon?

We must understand that what's needed daily is supernatural revelation by the Spirit to our hearts (Eph. 3:4 – 5). The truths of our faith aren't grasped by the natural mind. There are brilliant scholars who know the Bible but don't know Christ. If we want to fully experience Jesus, it can only be done through the Holy Spirit's ministry. Because of this fact, the apostle Paul prayed that his converts would be strengthened by more than his teaching — by the Spirit himself.

Paul had been in Ephesus for three years. While he was there, he taught them everything he could; he gave them the whole counsel of God. But once he moved on to plant churches elsewhere, he didn't stop thinking about them or stop praying for them. What's really incredible is that Paul believed God would grant them supernatural power through his prayers. Think how little we pray these kinds of prayers and expect God to do it. Think of the people we love and worry about but rarely pray for. Others we complain about or criticize, but sadly, we rarely take the time to lift them up to God.

**Is church about experiencing Jesus in a fresh way or merely hearing a great sermon?**

The Ephesians weren't the only people Paul prayed for. He did this for other believers too. To the Thessalonians he wrote, "Night and day we pray most earnestly that we may see you again and supply what is lacking in your faith." And "May he strengthen your hearts so that you will be blameless and holy in the presence of our God and Father when our Lord Jesus comes with all his holy ones" (1 Thess. 3:10, 13).

According to the Bible, Jesus Christ is going to return to earth. When he does, Christians need to be presented to him holy and blameless, washed in the blood, and strong in their faith. And Paul says, in essence, "That's what I'm praying for. I don't just teach you; I labor in prayer for you."

To the believers in Rome, Paul writes the following: "God, whom I serve in my spirit in preaching the gospel of his Son, is my witness how constantly I remember you in my prayers at all times" (Rom. 1:9 – 10). What a loving, devoted spiritual leader Paul was! Always remembering the believers, always interceding on their behalf. Maybe his prayers accomplished as much spiritually as his teaching did.

Now, think of this: Paul couldn't have prayed for all the believers by name. How could he have known everybody's name? There must be some way to pray, helped by the Holy Spirit, whereby he could bring groups of people to mind and pray for them. This is the type of intercessory prayer that we need more of in our churches. This is what will unite us together to receive God's strength and power.

## PASTORS NEED TO PRAY FOR THEIR PEOPLE

Sometimes on Saturday nights I imagine the audience I will stand before the next day in three Sunday services. That's thousands of people involved in intense spiritual warfare facing varied and complex problems that only they and God know about. They are fighting the good fight of faith, but the battles are hard. I cry to God for them that he might strengthen and encourage their faith.

Although I pray for my congregation, I look back and see a great lack in this area of my life. I have counseled and preached — a lot! But I haven't held up those precious people at the throne of grace as much as I should have. It's easier on the flesh to talk rather than fervently pray. Most pastors, I think, have failings along the same line as mine.

In his farewell speech at the end of his life, Samuel knew that the people had gone wrong. They had asked for a king and, in doing so, were rejecting God's leadership over them. King Saul would eventually bring trouble and loss to the nation. But instead of pouting and resenting people, Samuel reaffirms his steadfast concern for them. "How?" you might ask. He told them, "Far be it from me that I should sin against the LORD by *failing to pray* for you" (1 Sam. 12:23). In other words, he was saying, "I'm going to retire now, but I'm not going to retire from praying for you. It would actually be a sin against the Lord if I stopped praying for you."

How much spiritually stronger would our churches be if the leaders had Samuel's dedication? Or what would happen if the heart of Paul got into all the pastors, associate pastors, elders, deacons, and leaders around America? What kind of churches would we have? But instead of giving a prominent place to intercessory prayer, we have bought into the idea that "good Bible teaching" alone will solve everything. The country has a host of fine Bible teachers, many of whom are my valued friends. But with all our seminars, sermon series, and multiple versions of the Bible, can we honestly say the American church is spiritually strong and mature? Without prayer and the work of the Holy Spirit, teaching alone bears such meager fruit.

Paul seemed to believe that grace is poured out on others through intercessory prayer. When we pray for someone else, we are touching God with one hand and touching the person we care about with the other hand. Is there a more beautiful picture of the church, being the church, than to have one hand stretched up and the other stretched out?

Recently, I was in Belfast and then in London, speaking to hundreds of pastors in both cities. Both places are difficult fields for ministry. The pastors there face real challenges. I could have merely preached sermons full of scriptural truth and left it at that. I certainly did that to my best ability under God, but I knew all too well the discouragements and personal problems pastors faced. We all do.

That's why *I* wanted to do more than that. It was an honor and privilege for me to pray *with* them, and I have continued to have our church pray *for* them. When we believe in God and pray to him on behalf of someone else, God hears and will do as we ask. That sounds bold, but what else did Jesus teach? *Ask and you will receive. Seek and you will find. Knock and the door will be opened. When you pray, believe and you will receive.* If that's not all true, Jesus deceived us, and prayer is a waste of time. Unfortunately, many believers, including pastors, have secretly come to the conclusion that it is a waste of time.

But Delmis, as we saw earlier, did believe that God answers prayer. And she didn't just pray for herself; she ceaselessly prayed for her sister Karen to be released from the powers of darkness. Yet, even that wasn't enough for Delmis. She asked her youth group, its leaders, and her friends to pray for Karen. She didn't want Karen merely to come to church; she wanted Karen to have a relationship with Jesus.

Thirty minutes of Spirit-aided intercessory prayer is more

effective than all the new programs and stylistic changes we are constantly tinkering with. Human ingenuity can't be compared to God's power. Would the ministry of Eli and his sons have been different if they had prayed compassionately for their people? Of course, a selfish, greedy mind-set never is drawn toward secret prayer for the common people. But they are not our example! Jesus is when he intercedes for the disciples even though he's the one facing crucifixion (John 17:6 – 19). Paul is also our model as he prays for others even as he faces hardships, prison time, and angry opposition in city after city. Still he keeps praying for other believers.

## PEOPLE NEED TO PRAY FOR THEIR LEADERS

But let's reverse the question for a moment. How often do we pray for pastors, Christian leaders, and missionaries?

American Christians are really big on making sure our leaders get training from seminaries and leadership conferences, and I'm all for that. But Jesus actually said, "The harvest truly *is* great, but the laborers *are* few; therefore pray the Lord of the harvest to send out laborers into His harvest" (Luke 10:2 NKJV). Notice there who does the sending. Unless the Lord raises up men and women to do his work, all the seminaries in the world are useless. They can only train those whom God has set apart for the ministry. And Jesus said we should pray to that very end, "Lord, raise up laborers for the spiritual harvest we need."

**You may feel pastors don't need your prayers because they seem to have it all together spiritually. But you're wrong. Pastoring means facing immense and often mean-spirited challenges.**

Not only should people be praying for new leaders in our churches, but we also need to pray for our existing leaders. You need to pray for your pastor. By the way, if you don't have one, something is wrong! Sheep need shepherds, and God commands us to obey those who are over us in the Lord. You may feel pastors don't need your prayers because they seem to have it all together spiritually. But you're wrong. Pastoring in the twenty-first century means facing immense and often mean-spirited challenges.

Most pastors get emails that criticize them personally. People don't like what they wear, how they preach, or their sense of humor.

I wonder how much stronger pastors would be, and how much better at shepherding their flocks, if more folks prayed for them instead of criticizing them. Pastors have their own internal struggles, and they want God's blessing on their labors. But a few negative emails, personal criticism, or some church gossip can steal their energy and leave them feeling alone and fearful. What's really amazing is the hypocrisy of those who don't leave to find a "better" church for themselves, but keep attending every Sunday just to listen to a leader they love to criticize. Something is not right with that picture.

Preaching sermons isn't the hard part of being a pastor. In fact, find almost any pastor in America and put them in a corner with a passage of Scripture, and in fifteen minutes, they will come up with something to preach about. That's not the hard part. It's dealing with mean-spirited people; hearing the burdens of hurting men and women, often not knowing what to say; and counseling people who don't act on your counsel, and then seeing them return with an even bigger problem.

This happened to me recently. A couple of years ago, a young woman came in to visit me, and she was crying. She was pregnant and battling thoughts of having an abortion. "What should I do?" she asked. "I'm pregnant, and my boyfriend doesn't want me to have this baby."

I heard more of her story, and it was obvious the guy she was living with was not exactly of stellar character. "Listen, he doesn't care about you," I told her. "To him, you're just an object. When he wants you, he wants you, and when he's tired, he'll be gone."

I told her she needed to put her trust in Jesus and to hold on tight to him. But she wasn't sure.

"Please listen," I begged her. "I'm talking like a dad to you now. If you don't put your trust in Jesus, this won't be your last pregnancy. You'll probably have another baby, and then another one."

We prayed together, and I cried with her, but she didn't want to trust Jesus.

Three years later, she stood in my office once again. She was pregnant with her third child, had a different boyfriend, and was now overwhelmed by what her life had become.

"What should I do?" she cried.

It's not easy for pastors to walk through these kinds of things with people day after day. But most pastors do it willingly and lovingly. However, when they have spent the day counseling people only to open an email that talks about their pulpit style or the color of their suit, it can be wearying and hurtful. That's why pastors need the power and strength from the Spirit that Paul talked about. And Paul says that can come from the prayers of God's people. The great evangelist D. L. Moody insisted that the blessing on his ministry was due to an invalid woman who never ceased interceding for him.

Consider what Paul writes to the Ephesians: "Be alert and always keep on praying for all the Lord's people. *Pray also for me*, that whenever I speak, words may be given me so that I will fearlessly make known the mystery of the gospel.... *Pray* that I may declare it fearlessly, as I should" (Eph. 6:18 – 20).

Think of what Paul is saying. First, he reminds the people in Ephesus to pray not just for themselves, as much as they may need it, but to pray for other people in their church. And then Paul — *the apostle Paul* who had spent three years in Ephesus as their spiritual father, planted churches, wrote a third of the New Testament, and had a personal encounter with the Lord on the road to Damascus — *that Paul* said, "And by the way, while you're at it, pray for *me*."

If the great apostle needed prayer, how much more do I need prayer! How much more does the pastor in your church need prayer!

Paul said he needed prayer for the words he would speak. Often Paul took advantage of any situation to extemporaneously declare the good news of Jesus on the spot. By the way, it's interesting that no preacher in the New Testament (including Jesus) ever used notes. In fact, the apostolic preaching we have in the book of Acts indicates that they never knew they would even speak that day. No wonder they depended deeply on the Holy Spirit.

In addition to asking for the right words at the right time, Paul also asked for courage to fearlessly make known the mystery of the gospel. He was asking the fellow believers to pray for him so he would be bold, that he wouldn't fear the consequences of his words, and that he wouldn't leave out any parts of the gospel because they weren't popular with the people. Paul knew the danger of fear and compromise, so he desired the Spirit's strengthening. Paul believed the way for this to happen included others praying for him.

Unfortunately, too many of us don't do that. We're afraid to be vulnerable and say to other Christians, "Would you pray for me, because I'm in a battle and I need more of God's help?" Ministers are afraid to do that because it's just one more thing they might be criticized for or gossiped about. Seems like a sign of weakness, right? And yet Paul clearly asks believers to pray for him.

Paul didn't just ask the Ephesians; he wrote a similar request to the Romans. "I urge you, brothers and sisters, by our Lord Jesus Christ and by the love of the Spirit, to *join me in my struggle by praying to God for me*" (Rom. 15:30).

Think of the honesty expressed here.

Later on, in another letter, after nearly losing his life, Paul again admits how physically vulnerable he is. "He has delivered us from such a deadly peril, and he will deliver us again. On him we have set our hope that he will continue to deliver us, as *you help us by your prayers*" (2 Cor. 1:10 – 11).

When was the last time we leaders asked for personal prayer from God's people?

When was the last time you prayed for your church leaders without being asked?

In fact, dear reader, would you be embarrassed if I asked you when was the last time you prayed for people you say you love?

Earlier in this book, I talked about the need for leaders to love their people. I have no doubt that some readers looked at that chapter and thought of a loveless leader whom they knew. Perhaps as they read, they inwardly said, "You tell 'em, Jim Cymbala!"

While it is easy to point out flaws of those in charge, the most loving way to respond to someone else's shortcomings is to pray for them. The best thing we can do for our leaders is not to scold them, or even to take them out for Sunday dinner. What is better by far is to pray for them daily and fervently. How would our churches change if every day, every member prayed for their church's leaders? In one week we would feel and see the difference!

Many pastors leave the ministry, not because of the job, but because of the criticism they receive while trying to do their jobs. I've learned that we are good at criticizing and judging, but we're very slow to pray for people. May God stir up every congregation to pray for their pastor, because unceasing prayer rather than personal criticism is what's needed for all those in spiritual leadership.

I am one of the most blessed pastors I know, because I have lots of people praying for me. The Brooklyn Tabernacle Prayer Band is a special ministry in the church. Almost five hundred people come in assigned groups to the church from morning until night, praying for the needs that come into our church. They are also praying for me. That's their ministry. They pray for me when I am preaching on Sunday, and they pray for me when I am traveling. They always know my schedule. If I preach well and it blesses someone, who knows whether it had so much to do with me or almost everything to do with them? Perhaps when they cry out, "God, have mercy on him, help him, lead him, give him boldness, and give him strength," God hears their prayers and sends extra grace my way.

**May God stir up every congregation to pray for their pastor, because unceasing prayer rather than personal criticism is what's needed for all those in spiritual leadership.**

Do you believe this kind of prayer is possible?

If we don't, we might be orthodox in doctrine but quite unorthodox in Christian living.

## WE HAVE TO PRAY FOR EACH OTHER

In chapter 3 we talked about prayer, and if you read that chapter carefully, you will notice that most of the prayers I included there weren't prayers for me. It's not that I don't pray for things for myself; I do. Like everyone, I pray for God to bless me, to protect me, to strengthen me, and more. But the reason I included intercessory prayers is because the most intense and satisfying prayers I ever pray are the ones I pray for other people.

Recently, after being away, I had a huge stack of praise reports from the Prayer Band that had piled up on my desk. Seven or eight of them had the same thing in common: "Thank you, folks, for praying for my husband; he wasn't a believer, and he's now a Christian." "Thank you for praying for the person I asked you to pray for." Whether it was a friend, relative, or coworker, every one of them wasn't about the person who requested the prayer — it was about someone else. These people wanted to battle for someone else in prayer, and they wanted us on their prayer team. We have no idea what crushing circumstances others are facing. Can't we feel it in our own battles? Don't we care?

Other people in our churches, our communities, and our families need our prayers if they are spiritually asleep. Or they are weighed down with worry. Or they are drifting away from the Lord, dabbling with oxycodone or discouraged beyond belief. Tell me, who will pray for them if you and I don't? Especially for those who remain hardened to the message of Jesus. Will their hearts soften on their own? No. We must pray that God will visit them in tenderness and love.

No one is too far gone.

Everyone needs someone to persistently and consistently pray for them.

We also need to remember another awesome fact: We are never closer to Jesus than when we are interceding for someone else.

Do you know where Christ is right now?

According to the Bible, he is at the right hand of the Father, and he's making *intercession* for us. "Christ Jesus who died — more than that, who was raised to life — is at the right hand of God and is also interceding for us" (Rom. 8:34). And because Jesus is there interceding, "He is able to save completely those who come to God through him, because he always lives to intercede for them" (Heb. 7:25).

Did you know that while you were sleeping last night, Jesus was praying for you? He lives to make intercession. So when you and I get done with our ourselves, and we focus our prayers on other people, we are doing exactly what Jesus is doing: making intercession.

Can we grasp what kind of supernatural power there is in intercession?

How ministers and churches would be freshly blessed by God?

How struggling believers and those not trusting Christ could be changed?

For some people, intercessory prayer is their unique ministry. They might not even know it yet, but if they would just give themselves to it, they would be a spiritual powerhouse behind the scenes in the body of Christ! They might never hold a microphone and speak, but in heaven they will get a reward such as they can't imagine, because they were like Christ — intercessors.

What could be better than being on Team Jesus and interceding for others?

## TEAMWORK IN THE CHURCH

Now, I know some of you haven't remembered a word of this chapter because you only wanted to know what happened in that play-off game against UConn. We won! That meant we were one of the twenty-two teams that played in the NCAA Tournament that year.

We won that game, not only because we played as a team, but because we had each other's backs. Although we were of different races and ethnic backgrounds, we were committed to doing whatever it took to defeat the opposing team.

**Intercessory prayer is a grace that changes us, changes the people for whom we pray, and protects us and the church from the effects of the storms we face.**

What if, inside and outside our churches, across racial, denominational, and theological lines, we had each other's backs? What if we stopped majoring in the minors and instead majored in supporting one another?

What would happen if our churches united like that?

What victories would be won that today seem impossible?

Intercessory prayer is a grace that changes us, changes the people for whom we pray, and protects us and the church from the effects of the storms we face.

In college we played for the NCAA title (we didn't get it, we were eliminated in the first round), but as Christians we play for an eternal crown.

That's the crown we all want, and intercessory prayer is one way we in the church can say to one another, "I have your back."

## [ Chapter 11 ]

# A FOG OF CONFUSION

### Understanding the Old and New Covenants

T he Bible is confusing."

"It's boring."

"Sometimes, God seems cruel."

These are some of the comments I hear as to why people don't read their Bible more. When I dig a little deeper, I find that for some people, the Bible actually makes them question their faith — and not in a good way. They don't understand why certain contradictions seem to exist. Theologians might respond to their questions with scholarly articles, pointing out the original Greek and Hebrew meanings of the passages in question. Others, who have studied for decades, attempt to show deep underlying themes that help us reconcile seemingly contradictory parts of Scripture. And maybe they provide some good answers, but in many cases they just add to the fog of confusion.

Let me introduce you to Tito. Though he is a composite character and not real, he's like so many of the new converts we see at Brooklyn Tabernacle — full of awe and wonder at what God has done for him, but sometimes confused by what he reads in God's Word. If we are going to pierce through the fog and survive the coming storm, we will need to make sure that believers like Tito have the clear light and guidance they need to rightly understand Scripture.

## TITO FROM THE BRONX

Tito from the Bronx was quite a guy. He was born in Puerto Rico, but when he was young, his parents brought him to New York, where he grew up on the cold and uncaring streets of the city. His neighborhood was known for violence and gangs. A few of the kids in his neighborhood finished high school; none of them went to college.

Tito wasn't any different. He had an undiagnosed learning disability and struggled in school. He soon dropped out and turned to the streets, where he got involved with gangs and eventually got hooked on drugs. He became a dealer to pay for his habit.

He knew nothing about Christianity. He had been exposed to the voodoo of Santeria and its religious overtones when he was younger. Though Tito wasn't looking for God, God was looking for Tito. After Tito hit rock bottom with his drug habit, someone in his family brought him to our church. There he heard the good news of Jesus Christ, received Christ as his Savior, and was baptized at our church. He turned his back on his former life, and our staff helped him to start anew.

We also wanted to help Tito grow spiritually, so the New Convert Ministry workers handed him a Bible, so he could mature in his faith. He was told to read the gospel of John; but, of course, he wanted to explore the whole book. He developed his own reading pattern. It was a challenge due to his learning disability; but he faithfully stuck to it, reading a portion of the Old Testament in the morning and a portion of the New Testament in the evening. Christians around him were delighted with his ambitious reading plan and his desire to learn as much as he could.

Soon, however, Tito ran into problems. He often couldn't make sense of what the Bible was saying. Certain verses were confusing, and some of them seemed contradictory. Tito wasn't the first person to have this problem, but instead of setting the Bible aside like so many others, he came to us, seeking help and expressing his dilemma.

Tito met with a minister on staff and explained his confusion.

"I loved reading Jesus' words: 'Blessed are the merciful, for they will be shown mercy' [Matt. 5:7]. The kindness, gentleness, and love of Jesus is something I've never experienced before, and it makes me want to worship him even more! The problem is that in my morning readings, passages seem to contradict the idea that we should be merciful like him."

"What do you mean?" the pastor asked.

"Well, here it says that 'anyone who curses their father or mother is to be put to death' [Ex. 21:17]. Earlier in that chapter, I read that the Lord in pronouncing judgment had said, '... kill, without showing pity or compassion' [Ezek. 9:5]. This confuses me, because everything else I've read shows that Jesus was full of mercy."

Another day, Tito was reading the Psalms, and he came across the Psalmist crying out for deliverance from his enemies, yet he was asking not just for deliverance but *vengeance*. "Break the arm of the wicked man" and "Break the teeth in their mouths, O God" (Pss. 10:15; 58:6). To Tito, this seemed to be very different from the teaching of Jesus, who said, "Love your enemies and pray for those who persecute you" (Matt. 5:44). It reminded him more of a gang he had once been part of — the Latin Kings.

Tito knew he had a reading comprehension problem, so he would come to our staff with his questions. "Is the problem with me? Am I reading it wrong?" he would ask the staff.

On and on it went. Tito gave himself to careful study, but it led him into further questions. He read that God told Moses to teach all the commands that he had given him (Deut. 5:31), and the people should obey all of the commands (Deut. 12:28). Yet Tito read hundreds of commands given by God in the Old Testament that he knew Christians were not obeying.

One day he asked a man from the Midwest how farmers made a living every seventh year when they let their land rest fallow and unused. His friend informed him that no one did that, not even the Christian farmers. Tito was confused; in Leviticus 25:4, God clearly commanded that it be done. Soon Tito became aware that Christians didn't forgive the debts of anyone who owed them money in the seventh year, and yet that was in the Bible too (Deut. 15:1 – 2).

Another day, Tito read that Elijah had a triumphant encounter with the prophets of Baal on Mount Carmel when he represented God against their false teaching and idolatry. God heard his prayer and answered by fire, while the prayers of the false prophets went unanswered. This surely was a great victory for the forces of righteousness; but afterward, Elijah went into the valley and had all 450 prophets of Baal killed (1 Kings 18:40). "How does that apply to us Christians today?" Tito wondered. "Are Muslims and Hindus our enemies, and should they be dealt with the same way?"

**Tito never saw Jesus initiate any kind of vengeance against his enemies; although there were plenty of opponents to Christianity in the book of Acts, they were never threatened.**

Tito never saw Jesus initiate any kind of vengeance against his enemies; although there were plenty of opponents to Christianity in the book of Acts, they were never threatened. Instead, what impressed him was the story of Stephen being martyred in Acts 7. While being stoned, Stephen fell on his knees and cried out, "Lord, do not hold this sin against them" (Acts 7:60), asking forgiveness for the very people who were unmercifully killing him.

What did this mean?

Why was everyone in church disobeying God's clear commands?

And what should Tito from the Bronx do with all this?

Tito talked to Christians whom he had come to know in the Bronx, but they seemed to have no clear answer. In fact, they secretly admitted their own confusion as they read the Bible. Which was to be followed: the Law of Moses, or the words of Christ? The very spirit of the Old Testament seemed to be in opposition, in many ways, to the spirit of the New Testament, where grace and mercy prevailed rather than justice and vengeance.

One of the ministers at our church told me of Tito's difficulties and asked me to speak with him. I invited him to my office and began to tell him about how God had given us two covenants in the Bible. The first is called the Law, and the second, which *superseded* the first, is the covenant of grace through Jesus Christ.

I explained how the first covenant of the Old Testament is characterized by Moses and obedience to the Law. The second covenant centers on Christ and his sacrificial death for our sins. He asks us to trust him for salvation. I showed him in the book of Jeremiah how God differentiates between these two covenants: "'The days are coming,' declares the LORD, 'when I will make a *new* covenant with the people of Israel and with the people of Judah. It will *not be like* the covenant I made with their ancestors ... because they broke my covenant, though I was a husband to them'" (Jer. 31:31 – 32). This same passage is in essence repeated in the book of Hebrews in the New Testament, and the writer added, "For if there had been nothing wrong with that first covenant, no place would have been sought for another. But God found fault with the people and said: '... [the] new covenant ... will not be like the covenant I made with their ancestors'" (Heb. 8:7 – 9).

Tito began to understand the distinction between the two covenants. He saw that we are not Israelites, but passionate believers of God through faith in Christ.

Yet Tito revealed his continued confusion when he then asked me, "So are there two religions? And, if so, which one is for us?"

## WE ARE NOT OBEYING THE LAW

Tito isn't the only one who has questions. Sometimes, even believers who regularly study their Bibles meet confusion when sorting out exactly what applies to them as Christians. Recently, a woman came to my office for counseling. After a brief discussion about her work situation, she said, "My boss is acting so mean, I am going to pray an imprecatory prayer over him."

"What?" I asked in disbelief.

An imprecatory psalm is one that contains a prayer of punishment or retribution for the psalmist's enemies.

"I read it in the Bible. It said, 'Break the teeth in their mouths, O God' [Ps. 58:6] and 'Let death take my enemies by surprise' [Ps. 55:15]."

"Whoa, whoa, whoa!" I said, stopping her before she could continue. I explained to her that we don't do that anymore, that Jesus taught us to forgive our enemies and bless people who curse us.

In all sincerity, she looked at me and said, "But, Pastor, it's in the Bible."

What would you tell her?

How would you answer Tito's questions?

The fact is, nobody's obeying *all* the commands in the Old Testament.

In fact, most are casually ignored. So on what basis are we picking and choosing? I once asked one well-known minster for an answer.

"Well, um, you just know," he said.

I was stunned. How could I respond to that? The woman in my office obviously didn't know. Tito didn't know either. How could they know? Unfortunately, I don't believe that preacher knew either.

There has to be a better way.

**I don't think God intended for us all to become Bible scholars just to figure out whether we should punish or forgive those who have wronged us.**

Another well-known Bible expert told me, "All the commands have meaning. If you look at the whole teaching of the Bible, you can find a deeper, spiritual meaning."

He may be right. But I don't think God intended for us all to become Bible scholars just to figure out whether we should punish or forgive those who have wronged us. How would a new believer ever figure it out? I have questioned many seasoned believers who can't explain why they ignore hundreds of God's commands. But the confusion goes well beyond the commands of Old Testament Law.

"Praise God," the TV preacher says. "I'm in Cincinnati next month, and we're taking it for God. I'm claiming that land! Every place I put my foot is mine, hallelujah!"

But nowhere in the New Testament do we find the apostles (or Jesus) taking land. That's an Old Testament concept. Joshua took land. Paul never said, "I'm going to Macedonia, and I am claiming Macedonia for God." No. Christians win souls, not land.

To go a step further, circumcision of baby boys was given in the Old Testament as the essential sign of being part of God's covenant people. Disobedience to that command brought God's judgment. But the apostle Paul in one single sentence obliterates thousands of years of Old Testament ritual observance: "Neither circumcision nor uncircumcision means anything; what counts is the new creation" (Gal. 6:15).

Whether you are a Jewish believer or a Gentile believer, circumcision has nothing to do with our relationship with God through Jesus Christ. The new covenant is obviously different than the old covenant found in the Old Testament. But how do we know? What gives us the right to disobey some of the commands in the Old Testament? Or to cherry-pick some promises we like?

## HOW DO WE CHOOSE WHAT TO OBEY AND WHAT TO IGNORE?

Much mischief is created in Christian churches when leaders select commands and promises from the Old Testament and apply them to Christians living in a different age, even though they are not *found, taught,* or *illustrated* in the New Testament.

In the Old Testament, if the people obeyed God (which no one did perfectly anyway), he promised that victories would be won, the land would be possessed, and all enemies would be defeated. Only blessings would flow if the people stayed in right relationship with God. Only unconfessed sin would stop the march of triumph for God's people.

But things are much different in the New Testament, aren't they?

Apostles who were used mightily by God were thrown into prison and sometimes tortured and killed. This is clearly seen in the book of Acts. Jesus himself told us that if they persecuted him, they would also persecute his followers, for "a servant is not greater than his master" (John 15:20). The apostle Paul told Timothy, "Join with me in suffering for the gospel" (2 Tim. 1:8). When Paul and Barnabas were on their first missionary journey, they returned to some of the new churches they began, warning that, "We must go through many hardships to enter the kingdom of God" (Acts 14:22). This idea of taking up a cross and suffering for Christ in some way, shape, or form is not found in the Mosaic law. But today it is the experience of believers in Jesus around the world.

This is the error of the prosperity gospel, whose teachers selectively pick promises given to Old Testament Israel in the land and then apply them to believers in Jesus Christ living in our present era. They don't teach obedience to all the commands of that law system. In fact, they ignore much of it except for some materialistic promises that they know will sell to folks who don't know their Bibles very well. This is not rightly dividing the Word and does great harm when, for example, people lose their jobs and struggle financially. The response by these false teachers is, either you don't have real faith like theirs, or there's sin in your life.

Of course, many of these prosperity preachers are living large off the seed-faith offerings they procure from their followers. I have often wondered why, when their appeals for donations are made (with accompanying promises of ten-fold blessings), they don't say, "Give to *any* Christian cause, a missionary enterprise, or to your local church." Why does the money always have to go to the prosperity preacher if the formula is going to work?

Likewise, it is amazing how some teachers misapply the blessings and curses given specifically to Israel in the book of Deuteronomy. They triumphantly declare: "[We] will lend to many ... but will borrow from none. The LORD will make [us] the head, not the tail" (Deut. 28:12 – 13). But all of that was based on Israel's perfect obedience to the whole law. Who, among us, would dare claim that now?

Also, that is not the experience of Christians in the book of Acts — nor for the last two thousand years. Indeed, "we are more than conquerors through [Christ]" (Rom. 8:37), but our victory is not the physical kind of conquering army, but that of the apostle Paul who spiritually "ran the race," even though it included hardship and prison time.

> **The real spiritual meaning of the Sabbath rest is found not in a day, but through faith and fellowship with Christ. To Christians, every day is as sacred as the rest.**

So which is it? The material blessings promised in Deuteronomy, or the guaranteed hardships for followers of Jesus predicted in the New Testament?

All but one of the Ten Commandments are repeated and illustrated in the New Testament. Nowhere is Sabbath-breaking listed as a work of the flesh in the writings of the apostles. In fact, Hebrews 4 tells us the real spiritual meaning of the Sabbath rest is found not in a day, but through faith and fellowship with Christ. To Christians, every day is as sacred as the rest. Paul boldly declares that no one can judge us as to a Sabbath day (Col. 2:16), for we now have the reality of Christ — something Old Testament Israel never experienced.

It's not just Tito and the woman in my office who struggle with this question. New converts and even seasoned saints often find this quite perplexing. For a church that is in the middle of a storm, answering this question is critical. We must help new believers grow in the faith, and this confusion can be a roadblock to their maturing. In addition, critics often attack us for being inconsistent as we pick and choose the promises and commands we like.

## RIGHTLY DIVIDING SCRIPTURE

If we are to understand what we follow and why, we must distinguish between the two covenants. The apostle John helped us do this when he wrote, "The law was given through Moses; grace and truth came through Jesus Christ" (John 1:17). The entire Bible is "inspired by God" (2 Tim. 3:16 NASB) *but* it must be rightly divided. I have heard it was Martin Luther who once said that the hardest part of rightly dividing the Word of God is understanding the difference between the two covenants.

Looking through that covenantal lens, I was able to give Tito from the Bronx a simple rule to follow as he read the Bible, and I hope it will help all of us. The rule is simply this: No command or promise in the Old Testament can be applied to Christians today, *unless* it is found repeated and illustrated in the New Testament.

That sounds drastic, but in fact, it is what everyone is practicing, more or less. No Christian today obeys the command that God clearly gave to not wear garments made with two different fabrics (Lev. 19:19). No one I know forbids women, after giving birth, from coming to church to worship God, and yet that very thing was commanded in the Old Testament. Today, Christians who don't celebrate the Feast of Tabernacles don't feel they are missing anything, although it was one of the commanded holy days, given under Moses (Lev. 23:34).

This also gives us a clear response to the question asked by those outside of the faith, "Why don't you obey the hundreds of commands found in the Bible?"

We can confidently say, "I am a believer in Jesus Christ. I believe in his birth, death, and resurrection. I believe in the power of his blood that has cleansed me from my sin. I am a new creation in Christ. Whatever the New Testament teaches as a life that pleases God, I want to obey through the grace he gives me daily."

The New Testament is our main guide for the age in which we live, and the Old Testament must be read in light of it. A beautiful summary of all this is found, as stated earlier, in Hebrews 1:1 – 2: "In the past God spoke to our ancestors through the prophets at many times and in various ways, but in these last days he has spoken to us by his Son...." The final word God has spoken to the world is not Samuel, Joshua, Deuteronomy, or Leviticus. Old Testament passages are only properly used when they ultimately point us to Jesus and the New Covenant. The idea of Peter or Paul proclaiming a message that didn't end up with Christ and the new life he offers is impossible to imagine. "But we preach Christ crucified" (1 Cor. 1:23) was not a sermon series Paul preached for eight weeks; rather, it summarized the subject of his entire ministry. Our search must be for truth, yes, but especially "the truth that is in Jesus" (Eph. 4:21).

In Acts, the apostles were arrested and then miraculously set free by an angel. After that, a messenger from God gave them the following instruction: "Go, stand in the temple courts ... and tell the people all about this new life" (Acts 5:20). Notice that the apostles were told to go back and preach all the words of this "new life." That's what Christianity is essentially about — a new life! At the heart of it are not commands, but promises of the supernatural life of Christ in us, enabling us to live a life pleasing to the Lord.

Without Christ, how can we be saved from our sins?

Without "Christ in us," how can we be more like Jesus?

Sometimes we preachers can make detailed studies from the Old Testament and never return to the message of what's essential — all the words of this new life. Folks learn more about the commands and strictures of the Old Testament rather than the wonderful promises and truth of the new life that we have through Jesus Christ, his cross, and the promise of the Holy Spirit. We are not supposed to be preaching sermons that Moses and Ezra could have preached, for they never once mentioned the only name that brings life and salvation! Instead, we are to learn from Paul the apostle, who became "competent as [a minister] of a new covenant — not of the letter but of the Spirit; for the letter kills, but the Spirit gives life" (2 Cor. 3:6).

Even the letter of Holy Scripture can bring death unless it links us up to Jesus the Messiah. Remember that the Pharisees believed in one God, the Ten Commandments, divine creation of the earth, and the supernatural, yet they still ended up plotting the death of Jesus because of their spiritual blindness. The question then and now is still the same: What will you do with Christ?

In contrasting this new covenant of Jesus with the law that Moses received, (written on a tablet by the finger of God), Paul describes the law as "the ministry that brought death" (2 Cor. 3:7). He notes that "If the ministry that brought condemnation was glorious, how much more glorious is the ministry that brings righteousness!" (v. 9). Not many of us have fully accepted the fact that the Old Testament — with all of its glory, with Mount Sinai shaking, with thunder and flashes of lightning, with an awesome display of God's power — in the end leads only to condemnation and death.

Yes, it mightily convicts of sin, but the law of God offers no remedy or hope for our dilemma as sinners. It can only be a tutor or a schoolteacher to bring us to Christ. The reason for this is that "all have sinned and fall short of the glory of God" (Rom. 3:23). And once the law is broken, it requires punishment for the offender. No promise to do better and no amount of tears shed will reduce that ominous sentence one iota. "The one who sins is the one who will die" (Ezek. 18:20).

> The letter of Holy Scripture can bring death unless it links us up to Jesus the Messiah.... The question is still the same: What will you do with Christ?

Even if we could live a life of sinless perfection from now on, our condemnation is already assured by our past disobedience. But, praise God, all that has been changed for us by Jesus!

## HISTORICAL IMPACT OF DIVIDING SCRIPTURE

I am afraid some right-wing conservative Christians feel justified with their combative spirit by pointing to the Old Testament military general Joshua — who conquered Canaanite cities and sometimes left no human or animal breathing. But this is not the fighting spirit we are to have as believers in Jesus, the Lamb of God. Unfortunately, the so-called culture wars tend to make people militaristic and put them in an attack mode. But Jesus is the epitome of love, mercy, and compassion. This is why God says the new covenant of Jesus is not like the covenant he first made with the people of Israel.

Christians aren't supposed to "take back America" or conquer land for Jesus. Our aim is to see people experience salvation through faith in the gospel of Christ.

Those Old Testament images have nothing to do with the life we now live through faith in Christ. Muslims, Hindus, and others who oppose Christianity should not be considered enemies; in fact, they are part of the mission field God has placed before us as we try to share the good news of Jesus Christ. Indeed, we are taught to pray for the enemies of Christianity because they can become apostles the way Saul of Tarsus did.

Understanding this can help us advise the woman who came to my office because of problems with her boss. There is a real danger for all of us in drifting back into an Old Testament attitude of vindication and warfare instead of exhibiting the gentle mercy of Jesus. If we do drift back, we can end up misrepresenting the God who gave his Son in love to be our Savior.

One of the reasons Muslims will always resent Christians is because of the Crusades. Peter the Hermit preached the First Crusade in a spirit of Old Testament warfare and possessing land. The crusaders wrongly believed God cared about driving the Muslims out of the Holy Land, even when it meant killing men, women, and children. So when the crusaders wore crosses on their shields and took swords to kill Muslim men and women, their horrific misreading of Scripture defamed the name of Christ in Muslim communities for centuries.

Now, what the Muslims did to Christians was just as bad. But how could the crusaders wage a holy war — a Christian jihad, if you will — all in the name of Jesus, who would have deplored every ounce of it? People wearing the symbol of the cross were killing people Christ died for. And that same attitude still lives today in milder forms. Aren't you alarmed when you hear the anger and militancy in some of the so-called Christian political movements that seem devoid of the New Testament spirit of gentleness and compassion? Their justification is that they have a "righteous anger," but to most folks, it's just plain anger. I think the vitriol against gays and Muslims are two examples of that. We need to rediscover what it means to be "in Christ."

Consider Saul of Tarsus. He led the way in persecuting the church, hauling people into prison, and killing Christians. Some commentators believe that since the early believers would have remembered the Lord's command to pray for their enemies, Saul might have been the most prayed-for man on earth. Imagine, the most violent persecutor became the greatest apostle! I wonder what would happen if we would likewise pray for those who persecute us today?

A tragic, yet classic example of misunderstanding the difference between the covenants is seen among the Protestant reformers. Although bold men of great faith, they were confused when it came to handling those they perceived as adversaries to pure Christian doctrine. It was sad enough that they divided, wrangled, and dis-fellowshiped other believers who veered ever so slightly from their doctrinal convictions. But when it came to those labeled as full-fledged heretics, they shamed themselves and besmirched the name of Christ by their actions.

The famous John Calvin had one such "heretic," Michael Servetus, burned to death for daring not to accept Orthodox doctrine. Of course, no New Testament justification could be found for such a brutal act. Who can imagine Jesus or one of the apostles setting fire to another human being because they refused to believe God's Word? But Calvin (and other leading reformers who endorsed his decision) used Old Testament punishments against blasphemy to justify their cruelty.

As stated earlier, we need to consider Hebrews 1:1–2: "In the past God spoke to our ancestors through the prophets at many times and in various ways, but in these last days he has spoken to us by his Son." What God is saying today is that the truth is in Jesus. If we go to the Old Testament for teaching or edification, we must show its relationship to Jesus. Otherwise, we could easily create a distorted image of God, who can only be understood in the face of Jesus (Col. 1:15).

## REJOICE IN JESUS CHRIST OF THE NEW TESTAMENT
Mixing obedience to law as a way to merit God's favor is the exact opposite of salvation by God's free grace through faith in Jesus Christ. I myself grew up in a church that preached 80 percent law and 20 percent Jesus. The leaders believed there needed to be some law added to their message; otherwise, how would they frighten people into obedience and submission? But this legal foundation brings only condemnation and fear, because should you die unexpectedly, who knows if you had obeyed perfectly enough to go to heaven? Instead of understanding the full benefits of the new covenant in Christ, most in the church lived in a no-man's land between Jesus and Moses. Peace and joy escaped them because the terrors of the law constantly made them uneasy. They couldn't fully believe what Jesus meant on the cross when he said, "It is finished" (John 19:30), or understand that he had fully paid the price for all the sins we commit—past, present, and future.

Isn't it obvious to everyone that in the New Testament we are breathing different air? No longer is there an eye for an eye or a tooth for a tooth. But it is also a narrower way. Jesus said, "You've heard it written, 'Thou shall not kill,' but I say to you if you're angry at your brother and say 'Raca,' you've killed him" (Matt. 5:21 – 22, author's paraphrase). Our Lord is dealing here with heart motives that are deeper than mere actions. That's never found in the Law of Moses.

The new covenant says that if we look lustfully at a woman, it is just as if we slept with her (Matt. 5:28). Then again, the New Testament divorce law is much different from that under the Law. In the Old Testament you could divorce a person for any reason and remarry, but in the New Testament, only immorality and desertion are grounds for biblical divorce and remarriage (Matt. 19:9; 1 Cor. 7:15).

Although some Christians have little of this world's goods, they know that Jesus promised something better: an eternal reward. This is why early Christians were awaiting the return of the Son of God from heaven, because that's when their rewards and being with Christ eternally would commence. They knew their reward was not here. As Jesus said, "In this world you will have trouble" (John 16:33). That's a promise from him — a warning that is rarely mentioned, but it's the truth. However, waiting for us in heaven are immeasurable blessings, where every tear will be wiped away.

I recently had the honor of going to Hong Kong to minister to underground church pastors from mainland China. My friend Ravi Zacharias invited me to join him and some of his fellow apologists to minister over a series of days to hundreds of brave men and women, half of whom had served jail time for being a Christian. This, of course, would not seem odd at all to the apostles who were sent out by Jesus Christ. But it's a little unsettling to our comfortable Western mentality.

While I was sitting in the auditorium, I heard these brothers and sisters singing in Mandarin. I watched how they sang so wholeheartedly, many of them looking up toward the ceiling as if Jesus was five feet above them. I was deeply moved, because the building seemed filled with the holy presence of God. One particular melody was so strikingly beautiful that it caught my interest. I turned to my interpreter and asked, "Can you please tell me the lyrics of that song?"

He focused in and listened again and said,

> Oh, what they're singing is this: "Jesus, we love you for all that you have done for us. You came and died for us and gave your life, that we could be set free and have the gift of eternal life. So

now, since you have died for us, we offer ourselves to die for you, for that is only right. Since you gave your life for us, we will give our lives for you."

That was the gist of the song. Not the typical praise and worship song for a Sunday morning in America, right? But it's at the very core of the truth in Jesus: "If we suffer, we shall also reign with him" (2 Tim. 2:12 KJV).

The new covenant emphasizes heaven beyond any reward here on planet earth. Success in living and materialistic wealth are never mentioned in the New Testament as anything compared to what is waiting for us in heaven. Some mock that truth by saying it's the old "pie in the sky in the great by and by" religion, but we will all soon find out that "naked [we] came from [our] mother's womb, and naked [we] will depart" (Job 1:21). The true treasures that Jesus talked about are stored up for us in heaven, not on earth.

## IMPLICATIONS FOR OUR MESSAGES

I love the Bible so much, and we can learn from all of it, including the Old Testament. Over the centuries the Holy Spirit has at times used the Old Testament passages to give guidance to people seeking direction. There's wonderful truth in the stories of Abraham and Moses and especially the life of David. And there are phenomenal encouragements to faith as we study the trials of God's people. Even in this book you're reading, we have gleaned wisdom from Hannah's prayer and the life of her son Samuel. In addition, we find beautiful symbols, called "types," of Jesus Christ. One is found in the story of the Passover Lamb, where the blood was placed over the doorposts to provide protection and safety for those who remained in the house when God's judgment struck Egypt. Paul tells us that Christ is the final Passover sacrifice and believers are safe under the protection of his blood.

> Our church services must all be centered on Christ, who is our all-sufficient Savior and who has promised new life through his Holy Spirit.

But regardless of where our study begins, unless we end up getting to Jesus, our approach is deficient. Our church services must all be centered on Christ, who is our all-sufficient Savior and who has promised new life through his Holy Spirit. Only Jesus can make us the people God wants us to be. Demons are never afraid when we say "Jehovah" or "Creator" or even "holy, holy, holy." It's at the name of Jesus that they tremble. This is why the god of this world has stirred up such a frenzied attack against, not all religions, but specifically Christianity and the name of Jesus.

In summary, the new covenant is about spiritual realities: the invisible blessings of the new covenant, which include joy and peace and a sense of fulfillment in carrying out the purposes of God for our lives.

The Old Testament was primarily focused on material things: land conquered and occupied, good food, a beautiful temple in Jerusalem, enemies defeated (and even cursed at times), long life, and lots of children as a sign of God's favor.

Even Tito from the Bronx couldn't miss the reality that today most of the wealthiest people in the world are not Christians. Rather, they are people who do not believe in Christ — some of whom openly mock the thought of God and salvation from sin. In James 1:17 we see that every good gift comes down from above. If money and land mean so much, why is God giving them to people who reject him, while Christians in mainland China and in the Middle East live precarious lives with very little of this world's goods? It's because our reward is spiritual and internal, not material and external.

Once again, the simple principle I gave to Tito is helpful: No command or promise in the Old Testament can be applied to Christians today unless it is found repeated and illustrated in the New Testament.

Understanding this division can help those who are confused by what they read in the Bible, helping them to have a deeper awareness of what God wants from us and what God promises us. It can help us defend our beliefs to a culture that wants nothing more than to attack and destroy our faith. Most importantly, biblically literate congregations can better make and disciple new converts. We will see more lives transformed and rejoice as our churches grow from the inside out.

Rightly dividing Scripture matters in our walk and our talk. Understanding the differences between the new and old covenants will prevent Tito's confusion, the woman's imprecatory prayers, and the historical abominations that we have mentioned. The sooner we understand it, the more rest we will have in our walk with the Lord and the more clarity in sharing the good news of Jesus with others.

[ Chapter 12 ]

# ESCAPE FROM THE STORM

Mohammed's Story

*During a leadership conference at our church, I looked out at the attendees and saw a Middle Eastern man who stood out from the crowd — literally. Though we are a racially diverse congregation, the percentage of Middle Easterners is very small. But it wasn't his racial descent that prompted my notice — rather, it was his heart. That man, whom I will call Mohammed (not his real name), hadn't been coming to our church for long, but he had already made a big impression on all of us. I watched him hopping up and down with joy, singing praise songs, and waving his arms. Tears streamed down his face, and I could almost feel the emotion radiating from him. It was as if he was too happy for words to express.*

*Given the route Mohammed had taken to get to our church, his love for Jesus was understandable. While I didn't physically start bouncing where I stood, in my mind I was leaping for joy at what God had done in Mohammed's life.*

*Mohammed had grown up hating Jews and Christians — even celebrating their deaths. But as I watched him lost in worship that day, I could only marvel at the transformation that had taken place in his life. He was a modern-day Saul of Tarsus and, like Paul, one of the most fearless people I have ever known.*

*We have talked a lot in this book about a diluted gospel, but to me, Mohammed symbolizes the power of the good news of Jesus.*

*Mohammed had heard the gospel of Jesus while living in the Middle East and responded in faith to the message. He was discipled by excellent leaders from Lebanon, Syria, and the United States. Baptized by water at a church in Lebanon, he soon showed that he was a man whom God had specially called.*

*Not only does Mohammed understand the Scriptures, but he also can't wait to share the pure message of the gospel with others. In his radical departure from Islam to Christianity, Mohammed has confronted dangers and hatred that most of us could never fathom. And now here he was, bouncing up and down, joyously surrounded by a spiritual family that wants to do everything they can to support him and his ministry — many of them interceding in prayer for him daily. He is a marvelous example of walking through the storms of life through the enabling power of the Holy Spirit.*

## MOHAMMED

I grew up in a camp in Lebanon that was very different from what most Americans think of when they hear the word *camp*. This was not a camp with lakes, trees, and waterslides like those many American kids attend with their youth group.

The camp where I grew up was a refugee camp. After the 1948 Arab-Israeli War, Palestinian refugees who left their homeland were sent to refugee camps.

Some went to Syria or Jordan, but a majority, like my family, moved to Lebanon. There the Palestinians were given land, tents were erected, and my people were organized into formal refugee camps. By the time I was born in the early 1980s, the camps still existed, but the tents had been replaced by permanent structures. To this day, that is still where my people live.

As Palestinians, we wanted to hold on to our identity. We believed Israel was the enemy who had come into our land and taken it from us. And the United States had helped them. We were full of passion and love for Allah, but we hated the Israelis and were willing to die for the cause. Yasser Arafat, the founder and leader of the Palestinian Liberation Organization, also detested the Lebanese Christians.

We shared his beliefs, grateful to have someone to blame for our misfortunes.

Inside the camp, conditions were miserable and the refugees poor. As a people, we felt rejection from Lebanon, as well as the rest of the world. The United Nations was the only organization that provided us with any kind of relief. We suffered alone and felt abandoned, yet we lacked the resources to change our situation. There was little hope inside the camp.

The camps were run by the Palestinian militia, and most of the men worked for the militia. It was the only way to earn money. If you were to visit the camps, you would see boys as young as sixteen or seventeen carrying loaded weapons. Each of the eight-to-ten militias active in the camp had different tactics, but they shared one unified goal of fighting against Israel. My fathers and brothers found work with the various militias, and as a result, we always had a stockpile of weapons in our home. Every home in the camp had weapons. Fathers would give their young children a rifle and take pictures of them cradling guns that were larger than they were. It was something to be proud of.

I was the tenth of twelve children born to my parents. We were very poor, and when there was no work, there was no food. It was a depressing way to live. We were not allowed to work outside of the camp, yet there were no jobs in the camp. The only time the mood in the camp changed was when we heard about a bombing in Israel. If Israelis died in the bomb attack, the young people in the camp would gather in the streets to dance. The adults would pass out candy and sweets, and we would celebrate with a great party. On the night Israeli Prime Minister Yitzhak Rabin died, we celebrated all night long and didn't sleep until the party ended the next morning.

Those celebrations are so memorable to me because back then they were some of the few times I ever felt happy. I grew up in a family where I didn't feel loved by my father. He lived on the upper floor, separate from my mother and us kids, who lived on the lower floor. My father used to drink a lot, and at night he would come down and beat my mother. Night after night, we cried as we watched her suffer physical abuse. I remember once when my older brother fought my father to keep him off of my mother, but I was too young to do anything to stop him. I felt helpless.

My father was a tough man and well-known in our camp for his courage demonstrated in one daring night raid. I was only two or three years old when it happened, and I heard about it first from my teacher at school; later, my mother confirmed the details.

As part of his militia duties, my father would lead groups of young men into Israel. Because land mines were a real threat, when they entered Israel, they would take mats and walk on them, so the land mines wouldn't explode. They had finished one of those nighttime operations, and my father took off his jacket and hung it on a tree before he went to sleep. When one of his guys went missing in the night, the others in the group woke up my dad because he was their leader. They believed that the missing young man might be a spy, and they feared he would inform the Israelis of their whereabouts. Minutes later, they heard a plane circling overhead. My father told the group they needed to leave immediately, and they all ran.

All of the young men made it back to camp, but my father didn't. The area they had just left had been bombed, and my father was assumed dead. His picture went up all over the camp, and they built a memorial in his name. Six days later, he walked back into camp, but because he had left his jacket hanging on the tree with his ID card still in it, it was feared that my father's name was in the Israeli records. He was now wanted by them.

As a result of his exploits, my father became very famous around the camp. Everyone was so proud of him — he was a local hero because he had almost died a martyr and returned to talk about it. When my teacher initially told me about that, I couldn't believe it, and I asked my mother to tell me the story. When I heard the details, I was also proud of him!

Yet I don't think my father was ever proud of me.

Never once in my life did he hug me, compliment me, or tell me he loved me. I never once heard him say, "Happy birthday, son!" I didn't even know what day my birthday was until I was in my mid-twenties and had left the camp.

My brothers teased me when I was young, saying I was an "imam chaser." Whenever I saw a Muslim imam, I would go running after him. In the summer we had Muslim school — similar to vacation Bible school for children in the United States — and I would study under the guidance of the imams. I loved Islam and was fortunate to have a Wahhabi mosque — an ultraconservative branch of Sunni Islam — right next door to us. They encouraged me to study and learn Sharia law. But my father didn't approve. "It's all false teaching! They are too strict!" he would say.

My older brothers didn't approve either. They would make fun of me, saying, "What, are you going to come home looking like an imam tomorrow?"

My father died when I was twelve. When I turned fourteen, I finally felt free to go ahead and do what I wanted. So I began studying regularly with the Muslim imam. He introduced me to the Koran, and we studied the sayings of Mohammed. The Wahhabi beliefs were extreme; for example, a Muslim who did not pray was considered an infidel. Those who followed the Wahhabi ways would try to convert Muslims who didn't believe the way they did, and if they refused to convert, the Wahhabi believers could try to kill them. It was all very radical and hate based.

The more I learned, the more radical I became. My brothers continued to taunt me for spending time with the imams. They weren't religious and didn't want a religious person in our home. "How are you going to make a living off of that? There's no money in that. You'd be better off going to school or getting work with the militia!"

My relationship with them had never been good. In our culture, the older brothers have authority and control over the younger brothers. I had been taught to respect them just as I had respected my father. If I disobeyed them, I got a beating — sometimes, a very bad beating. Soon I felt that even my older brothers were infidels, but I didn't have the courage to tell them.

Despite their opposition, I continued to study with the imam. One day, when I was at his house for lessons, I discovered he had a New Testament. I picked it up, and the imam immediately told me to put it down. He forbade me from reading it. I did as I was told. My lessons with him continued, and eventually he trusted me so much that he gave me the keys to the mosque. I would open it for morning prayer, and some days I would lead prayers five times a day. I began wearing a long white gown, and I grew a beard. By then, I was sold out to the Wahhabi way of life.

One day, when outside of the camp, I found myself in an area of the Lebanese territory where both Muslims and Christians lived. A man approached me. He started telling me about Jesus Christ, and I was immediately offended. *Who is this guy? Can't he see by my dress and my beard that I am a good Muslim? Why would he tell me about Christ when we're the ones who have the truth?*

He introduced himself as George. There was something different about him. The way he spoke to me was different from the way we spoke to people we wanted to convert. George seemed to come from a place of love, not hate. He had a peace I didn't have. Several times he offered me a New Testament, but I rejected it. When he offered me a tract, I finally relented. I read it when I got home. It was about Jesus Christ, and it said something very disturbing — that Jesus claimed to be the Son of God.

Tucked inside the tract was an invitation for a celebration. The caption read, "Come Celebrate Joy and Peace." I decided to go, but when I arrived, I discovered no one else was dressed the way I was — like a good Muslim. I quickly realized it was a Christian celebration, and I turned to leave. Before I could go, George stopped me. He and several of his friends began to talk to me about Jesus. I used to hear Christians at mass, but George and his friends were different from them. I felt as if they truly cared about me — something I hadn't experienced much in my life. In fact, they seemed to *love* me. That alone was confusing.

Why do they love me, while I hate them? How can they find such joy and peace worshiping their God? Why don't I experience that?

They offered me a New Testament, and this time I took it. Not because I believed what they were saying, but because I wanted information. My curiosity about the New Testament had only grown since I had first seen a copy at the imam's house. I wanted to read what was in it, so I could understand what Christians believed. I also wanted to look up some of the verses that were quoted in the tract. I thanked them and left. But before I returned to the camp, I hid the New Testament under my religious gown.

At home, I closed all of the doors and windows to my room. I was fortunate to have my own room since my dad had passed. Once I was certain it was safe, I began reading. It was a strange experience for me. The New Testament was like a story, not at all like the Koran. I read a little bit that day, but the next day I had a desire to know more. I knew it was wrong, but I began reading the New Testament every day. As I read, I realized that it talked a lot about peace and joy, loving and caring for other humans. It was shocking to read that Jesus told his followers to "love your enemies," "bless those who persecute you," and "do good to those who persecute you."

Though I was inexplicably drawn to the words of the New Testament, I remained a good Muslim. I went to the mosque every day and continued to lead prayer five times a day. My god, Allah, whom I believed to be the true god, said that we should kill Jews and those who are polytheists. We are to curse Jews and Christians and all those who don't believe in the teachings of the Koran.

Muslims refer to Jesus as Isa, and I remembered reading about Isa in the Koran. I started paying more attention to what the Koran said about Isa now that I was also reading the New Testament. I could see that even in the Koran, Isa was completely different from the rest of the prophets, and even from Mohammed. In the Koran I read that one of the miracles of Jesus was that he started speaking as an infant and that he went on to raise people from the dead. But what struck me the most was that he used his power to do *good*. Everywhere he went, Jesus did good things such as healing the blind, the lame, and the lepers. None of the prophets, even Mohammed, did what he did.

Though the teachings of the Koran didn't exactly match the information I was reading in the New Testament, I noticed some startling similarities, such as the fact that a crucifixion is described in the Koran — though it doesn't say that it was Jesus who was crucified. I also found a Koranic verse that said, "Peace upon me when I was born, when I died, and when I was sent up." After studying about Isa in the Koran, I had even more questions.

Muslims believe that Jesus, not Mohammed, will come back at the end of time and judge the world. Why do Muslims believe it will be Jesus and not Moses or someone else? The Jews are also waiting for their Messiah, and the Christians are waiting for Jesus to return in a second coming. Why are three religions waiting for Jesus?

I met with George and his friends, who were now my friends too, and I asked them questions. They were patient and kind and gave me additional booklets to read. I sneaked their materials back into the camp, and in the secrecy of my room I read them all. When I finished, I hid them under my pillow.

I continued to practice Islam, but I began to struggle with my faith. I thought I had all the answers, but the questions kept coming, until I was no longer sure that as a Muslim I had the truth on my side. Finally, I decided to ask the imam I studied with some of my questions. Immediately he was suspicious.

"Why are you asking questions about Isa and the Christians?" he demanded.

It had been a year and a half since I had gotten the New Testament from George, so I told the imam everything that had transpired.

"Did they give you money so you would become a Christian?" he asked.

"No."

"Did they have you drink coffee or tea?"

"Yes," I said, but I had to stop and think. Muslims in our culture believed it is possible to do acts of magic or cast spells through drink.

"See, they have put a spell on you!" the imam insisted—and I believed him. Surely, it was possible.

The imam had me lie down on the ground, and he and the other imams began reading the Koran over me. They videotaped the entire experience. They came to my room and confiscated all of my reading material, including the tract, the booklets, and the New Testament. They replaced those items with Muslim apologists' teachings and stories of priests and Christians who had converted to Islam.

They began to visit me more and tried showing me the love and friendship that I had described with the Christians, hoping I wouldn't return to those people. At the same time, they were doing it to keep watch on me. They didn't want anyone to know what had happened to me—they wanted it to remain a secret. But their love didn't feel authentic. One imam told me that if I ever visited with the Christians again, he would shoot me in the foot. This somehow did not seem very loving to me!

I continued to go to the mosque, but my prayers changed. Instead of praying as the Muslims prayed, I would pray, *Lord, show me the truth*. I was struggling, because my eyes had been truly opened and I wasn't sure what to do with what I now knew.

Several weeks passed, and I decided to attend another Christian meeting like the ones I had attended in the past. It was located far from our refugee camp. Once I got there, I told them of the confusion within me and my talks with the imam. "I believe in Christ—just not

100 percent — but I can't come to any more Christian meetings after this," I told them. They responded by encouraging me to give my life to Christ and promised that they would help me in my struggles. So on July 14, 2000, I gave my life to Jesus Christ. One of my friends gave me a New Testament and told me I must read it so I could grow in my faith.

When I returned home, my brother met me at the door. "Where were you?" he asked. Then noticing my pocket, he asked, "What's in there?"

He snatched the New Testament from my pocket and became furious when he saw what it was. Despite the fact that the imams didn't want the word to get out about what was happening with me, they had told my brother so he could keep an eye on me. My brother believed people were already talking about us — in our culture, that could get you blacklisted — and now he had evidence.

"You have brought great shame on our family. Why are you doing this? Why are you attending these meetings? You're free to do what you want, but if you go back to these meetings, I will kill you."

My mother came to see what all the commotion was about. When I told her, she started weeping. "This is a shame over our family!"

Suddenly, I started to feel ashamed. Their questions continued, and I didn't have answers for them.

"What is this new revelation you have," my brother asked, "that the God of the universe would come to earth in human form and be like us humans? Did he use the bathroom like a human?"

This was a standard question that Muslims used to attack Christians. It was hard to believe that the God who created the world would have to use the bathroom. I had no answer for his question, so I said what I could.

"I know the truth."

"So tell us what the truth is," he mocked. "And is it just you who has the truth? Out of all of the people in the universe, you received this revelation and you know what the truth is? Everyone else who follows Mohammed is wrong? Is that what you're saying?"

Soon my other brothers joined in the attack. They had the wrong perception of Christians, and they now thought I was one of them. At one point my brothers tied me in chains and took me up to the roof. My mother would come up to speak with me and break into tears at what was happening. No one in my family wanted anyone to know what was happening, because they were so ashamed of my behavior. Eventually they released me from the chains and brought me downstairs. The imams came back, promising me things that every man in the refugee camp wanted — a business or the opportunity to leave the country — because they thought the Christians had some kind of financial hold on me.

The pressure continued to build until one night, I escaped. I went to the church I had visited, and I knocked on the door. The pastor answered, and I told him what had happened, and I began to cry as I thought of my mother and what might happen to her when people found out. I knew she could be tortured or killed.

Likewise, the pastor and members of his church were afraid for me and themselves. They locked me in a room for two days and wouldn't allow me to leave while they tried to come up with a plan for me to move from Tripoli, the second largest city in Lebanon, to the capital — Beirut. The fear in their eyes was unmistakable; they knew the consequences could be death if they were caught helping me.

A few days later, we took the hour-and-a-half trip north, along the coast. In Beirut, I was taken to a theological seminary in the city. The president of the seminary had heard there was a Muslim seeker who had been studying the New Testament for a year and a half, and they had been praying for me and hearing reports of my journey to Christ.

I asked if I could use a phone to call George and his friends to let them know I had arrived safely in Beirut, and that's when I learned the terrible news. My address book had been confiscated by the imams when they removed the reading material from my room. My brothers had gotten ahold of the information and figured out it was George who had led me to Christ. They showed up at his house and threatened him and his family. "If you don't return our brother to us, we're going to kill you!" They apparently thought I was hiding at George's house.

George's family was Orthodox Christian, and they feared for their lives because of George's evangelistic efforts to reach Muslims. Terrified of losing their son, or their own lives, George's parents sent him to Brazil, where he still lives today.

I understood how George must have felt in Brazil. Having spent twenty years myself rarely stepping outside of the refugee camp, being in Beirut was like being in a foreign country for me. Suddenly, I was living among the Lebanese whom I had hated in the past and who had always hated Palestinians. I had no friends. Muslims wanted nothing to do with me, and Christians were afraid of me. I was living on the top floor of a renovated church with no electricity or natural gas. The room was nothing more than a ceiling and walls with a windowless hole, so I could look outside. I showered with a hose connected to a cold-water faucet.

Despite my outward circumstances, I experienced true peace and joy for the first time in my life. I would sit in bed and listen to worship music and read my Bible. One day a pastor recognized my spiritual development, and he and his daughter accepted me into their home and their family; and that seemed to make them genuinely happy. One of the happiest days of my life was when he said to me, "I have a daughter, and now I have a son."

God had replaced my earthly father who had died with a man who became not only my spiritual mentor, but also my confidant, friend, and the loving father I'd never had. I attended church several days a week, and he continued to help me grow in the faith. In 2001, I was baptized at the church. As a further outward sign of the changes that had occurred inside of me, I shaved my beard.

While freedom of religion was ostensibly practiced in Lebanon, and both Christians and Muslims could worship as they chose, it was not acceptable for a Muslim to convert to Christianity. In some way, I had defamed Islam. As a result, I was often targeted and thrown in jail. They never said it was because of my faith — they always claimed it was because of something else — but I knew why I was behind bars. Yet I used that time as an opportunity to tell other inmates how much Jesus loved them.

As word of my story got out, I was invited to share my testimony at a retreat in Cyprus. Because I had been born in the refugee camp, I never acquired citizenship papers, only travel documents, so I was concerned when I had to apply for the visa. The man behind the desk immediately recognized the disconnect between my name and my travel plans.

"Why is a man named Mohammed going to Cyprus for a Christian retreat?" he asked.

I shared my testimony with him, and surprisingly, he was encouraged by it and granted me the visa.

My trip to Cyprus was the first time I had ever been out of Lebanon. During one of the breaks in the retreat schedule, I went outside to take photos of the beautiful mountainous area. As I looked through my lens, I felt a strong pull or connection with a certain house. It felt like a divine pull, so I walked over to investigate. Once there, I met the owner, and he invited me in to have coffee with him and his wife. I told them a little bit about myself, and then they shared about their lives. They were originally from the United States, and he said he was a minister of the gospel — and he was *Jewish*.

Though he was a Christian and from America, I had spent my entire life hating the Jews, and this was the first time I had ever met one in person. I grew flustered, not sure what I should say or do. But he put his hands on me and started praying, and I felt something in the room. I knew the Holy Spirit had brought me here to meet this man.

"Would you be willing to come and share your testimony at a discipleship school where I serve?" he asked.

I agreed.

A few days later, he took me to the discipleship school for Messianic Jews. We walked in, and I saw decorative menorahs and young people worshiping God in English. But one man in the room didn't seem to fit in with the rest of the crowd. I asked about him and was told he was an Israeli.

"There are five more Israeli Christians here with him," my host said. He had no idea what affect that had on me.

My heart raced and my chest tightened, making it hard to breathe. My skin tingled, and I felt a cold sweat forming on my skin. I couldn't believe I was standing in the same room with an Israeli. I had never met one; I had never even seen an Israeli in real life — only on television. But I knew all about them. These were the people who kicked us out, stole our land, and forced us into the refugee camp. Every bad thing in my life was because of the Israelis. I was stunned to find myself standing just a few feet away from one. I could feel the hatred welling up inside of me when my host introduced me and asked me to share my testimony.

I kept my eyes on the Israelis as I spoke. They listened attentively as I spoke, occasionally nodding in agreement. I could feel my hate thawing and the love of God radiating from them, even though I was Palestinian.

When I finished speaking, they gathered around me and one of them said, "Mohammed, in the name of all the Jewish people, we are sorry. We love you, and we want to ask for your forgiveness," and then they said something so startling, I couldn't even bear hearing it. "We would like to wash your feet."

I ran to a wall and leaned against it, weeping.

They came over and repeated their request again. Through my sobs, I said, "I understand that you love me, but don't wash my feet."

But they insisted. They made me sit down, and while one of them washed my feet, the others laid hands on my head and started praying for me. I watched as the Israeli man gently picked up my right foot, and I could see that he was weeping too. As he gently scrubbed the bottom of my foot, I felt as if God was also doing a cleansing — of my heart. While the Israeli washed the sole of my foot, God washed every bit of hatred out of my soul. The hatred was replaced by love, not only for the men in the room, but for all Israelis. And I began to weep even harder.

Then I asked the men praying over me, "Please, can you pray in Hebrew?" I knew that only the Holy Spirit could have arranged for this moment. God was so real to me as I, a Palestinian man, sat in the chair, having my foot washed by an Israeli Christian, while his friends prayed blessings over me in Hebrew.

Over the next few years I had the opportunity to share my testimony in evangelical and Orthodox churches, to travel and speak and tell my story on Christian television.

When one of the TV programs I was on aired in the camp, my family was able to see the entire broadcast, in which I shared the truth about Islam and also the gospel of Christ. My sisters later said to me, "You are a good man. The only thing bad about you is that you are a Christian."

Years earlier, I had tried to visit my mother and my sisters, but when I went back home, one of my brothers pulled a gun on me. After the show was broadcast, their anger only increased. Resentment filled the refugee camp, even though I had been gone for years. On the camp's website they started writing things, including death threats of "We'll crucify you!" and they pronounced a fatwah (a legal decree) on me.

I haven't been back since.

However, in 2007, my mother was ill in a hospital outside of the camp, and I visited her there. We talked, and after seeing me on TV, she chose to accept Jesus as her Lord and Savior, shortly before she passed away. I was overjoyed now at the assurance that we would spend eternity together. Unfortunately, I was prevented from going to her funeral, and my family denied that she ever accepted Christ. But I know that my mother is with the Lord.

As I grew bolder in my faith, I began to testify more strongly about my leaving Islam for Christianity. This angered not only the Muslims in the refugee camp where I once lived, but Muslims everywhere. Eventually, the persecution was so bad that I was granted asylum in the United States. While I love this country, I don't plan to stay long. My heart is in the Middle East with my family and my people. I hope to return one day to proclaim the message of peace and joy in Jesus to every Muslim God helps me to reach. Though my family may say I am an infidel because I have become a Christian, that is not the truth. I have found Truth, and I want them to find Him too.

Though I have gained a new spiritual father here on earth and an eternal Father in heaven, and though I am surrounded by my Christian brothers and sisters, I long for my biological family to join my spiritual family. I do not hate my brothers and sisters; instead, I long to see them in heaven. But I cannot renounce what I know to be the truth. In Matthew 19:29, Jesus promised, "And everyone who has left houses or brothers or sisters or father or mother or wife or children or fields for my sake will receive a hundred times as much and will inherit eternal life."

I feel as if I have already received so many of the rewards Jesus promised.

As a Palestinian, I felt rejected by the entire world, but today I know I am loved by the Lord Jesus Christ. In the past I didn't have any hope — only limitations; but today my hope is in the Lord. In the past I wanted to serve a god that I didn't know; but today I serve Jesus, who is also my Brother, my Friend, and the One I love most of all. In the past, if I had a problem, I wouldn't know where to go; but today I know where to go for help. God is my stronghold, and I can run into his presence. In the past I used to do things trying to earn God's favor; but now I live out of love for the God who first loved me.

Though Satan has done his best to stop me, before I left the Middle East, I was privileged to lead scores of Muslims to Jesus and see them be baptized. I even started my own ministry, providing them with conferences and a center where they could learn English and also safely learn more about Christ. I remember how I was brought to knowing about Jesus Christ through George and his friends, who boldly shared their faith despite the danger that surrounded them. I want to do the same. While I am thankful to be in the United States and surrounded by so many loving Christians in Brooklyn, I cannot wait to get back to the Middle East. I know now that there are many believers all over the world praying for the Muslim people to come to know Christ. I desire to be part of that happening.

I once wanted to kill Christians, but now I am ready to die for the cause of Christ. The hate I once felt has been replaced by love, not only for the Palestinians in the camp, but for the Jewish people as well. Though I once celebrated their deaths by dancing in the street, absorbed radical lessons of hate from the Muslim imams, and led prayers in the mosque five times a day, I now wear a Jewish menorah pendant around my neck and pray for these people.

Muslims aren't attracted to Jesus so much by theological arguments as when they sense his love in us. Had George not spoken to me lovingly about Jesus, right now I would probably be dead or in prison for killing Israelis. If God can use George to reach a man like me, I know he can use me to help those who are just like the old Mohammed.

## THE POWER OF THE GOOD NEWS ABOUT JESUS

What an amazing story! From hatred and violence to having his feet washed by his former archenemies. It reminds me of the conversion of Saul of Tarsus, the violent persecutor of the early Christians, who met Jesus and had his life transformed. Saul was steeped in the teachings of the Pharisees, but God used him later to bring the gospel to Gentiles throughout the Roman Empire. Those he had formerly looked down upon now became precious to him because of the love of Christ in his life. This is what God has done in Mohammed's life.

How did this all happen? It was, as always, the power of the good news about Jesus working in Mohammed's heart as he received it in simple faith. This kind of testimony was the norm as Christianity spread and its churches grew. This was the *new life* that was the message of the apostles — a radical new beginning for everyone who trusted Christ and his death on the cross.

What was commonplace then, and also during seasons of spiritual renewal over the subsequent centuries, has become unfortunately less common today. We sometimes hear of church attendance spiking upward at a church, or hear of the communication skills of a noted teacher, or hear of a new state-of-the-art facility. But what we too seldom hear is the testimony of a dramatic life-change because of Jesus and his salvation. If our Lord could transform a Mohammed, won't he do the same in our churches and through our individual lives as we share Jesus?

George told Mohammed about the good news of who Jesus is and what he did on the cross. The Holy Spirit anointed George and shed light into Mohammed's darkened mind. George and his friends prayed for Mohammed and showed him Christlike, unconditional love. Human talent and expertise weren't part of this miracle. They are not what Christianity is really about. Jesus and his love are all we need to help us walk through the storms of life.

# Chapter 13

# COMING ON THE CLOUDS

Preparing for Christ's Return

When Superstorm Sandy hit New York City with ferocious power in 2012, it didn't come as a surprise. Sophisticated meteorological instruments had been tracking Sandy ever since she formed on the other side of the Atlantic Ocean. For several days there had been warnings about her arrival as her strength and speed were constantly being monitored. The weather forecasters were even able to pinpoint to the hour her arrival that coincided with that evening's high tide. What they had failed to predict was the amount of damage that occurred as a result of the collision of the storm and the tide — and it was the tide that caused the lights to go out in Lower Manhattan.

But I want to remind you there is another arrival that all of us will experience — and not just those living in New York City or even in America.

One day in the future, Jesus Christ will come back to the earth he left two thousand years ago. But unlike Sandy's arrival, when Jesus comes back, there won't be any warning at all.

Since he proved himself to be God's Son by rising from the dead, we can be absolutely sure of his promised second coming when he said, "You will see the Son of Man sitting at the right hand of the Mighty One and coming on the clouds of heaven" (Mark 14:62).

The return of Christ, sometimes called "the day of the Lord," will come as a surprise to the inhabitants of earth. "For you know very well that the day of the Lord will come like a thief in the night" (1 Thess. 5:2). There isn't a thief anywhere in New York City who sends a text message giving his victims the expected time as to when he will break in. Likewise, the coming of our Lord will occur at the least-expected time.

The return of Jesus will mark the end of "time" as we know it and usher in eternity. These are hard-to-imagine facts, but they are foundational to our Christian faith. Our life on earth is transient, but what looms before all of us is an eternity — either with Jesus in heaven or away from his presence. Therefore, the suddenness of Christ's return calls for two requisite attitudes in our minds.

The first is one of spiritual readiness. "So you also must be ready, because the Son of Man will come at an hour when you do not expect him" (Matt. 24:44). We must continue to live in close fellowship with Christ so "we may be confident and unashamed" when he returns (1 John 2:28). This requires living daily in his Word and walking by the Spirit so that we can resist the seductive voices that tell us to "eat, drink and be merry" (Luke 12:19), for there's nothing beyond the grave.

The second important mind-set is to remember the brevity of our lives. Like Christ's return, we don't know the day or time of our death. But we do know that there will be a final moment to all of our lives, and at that time there will be no going back and fixing things. We will not have a second chance at living better. There will be no occasion for further witnessing for Jesus; no opportunity to again pray for a loved one; not another chance to encourage a struggling soul; and no more chances to be light in the dark world God rescued us from.

Our time is fixed and shorter than most of us think. As I write this book, my mother is a week away from her ninety-ninth birthday! Yet the Word of God calls even her long life a wisp of a vapor compared to the endless eternity lying before her.

So what shall we do?

Despite the storm we are in and the statistics that show the sad plight of Christianity in America, the future is as bright as our faith in God. His promises help us remain fixed despite the storm, that's for sure. Gathering up what we have covered together in this book, here are a few obvious action items we can take in order to see dramatic, God-inspired change around us.

**First, let's discover in a fresh way the practice and power of prayer.** When Hannah couldn't take her childlessness any longer, she broke through into a new dimension of intense, faith-filled praying. Let's use our dissatisfaction with the barren status quo as an impetus to go to God's throne of grace and not give up until he responds with new spiritual blessings. Remember, it doesn't matter how spiritual you feel on a given day. Access to the Father is always and only through the shed blood of Jesus. That alone brings us near.

We need to give ourselves to prayer individually and corporately. Jesus categorically stated, "My house will be called a house of prayer" (Isa. 56:7; Matt. 21:13), so he obviously wants us to know that prayer is foundational for those who belong to him. Because of Christ's words, I encourage every believer in a prayerless church to approach the leadership and find out why prayer is not given top priority. God certainly recommends it everywhere in his Word, and he wants us reminded that his ear is always open to the petitions of his children.

My guess is that most pastors would love the encouragement of believers who want to intercede for others and petition God for more of the Holy Spirit's blessing. Just imagine what might happen if prayer meetings started springing up in local churches everywhere and Christians began to pray as never before! Would God turn a deaf ear to the fervent, Hannah-like prayers of sincere, seeking believers?

That's utterly impossible if the Bible is true.

If the pastor maintains he is committed to a "different model" than the one found in the New Testament, then maybe the Lord will lead you to form your own prayer group, or possibly you need to look for a different, more biblical church. Life is brief, and there is no time to suffer frustration on such an important matter.

> **Imagine what might happen if prayer meetings started springing up in local churches everywhere and Christians began to pray as never before!**

**Second, let's search the Scriptures and learn more about the Spirit of God.** We can't stay stuck in denominational or traditional modes of thinking that often deny and negate the presence of the

Lord. The Bible is our only guide, and God "rewards those who earnestly seek him" (Heb. 11:6).

The stronghold among us that must be broken is a form of godliness (religion) that simultaneously denies the power of the Spirit. It's not a Baptist, Reformed, Lutheran, charismatic, evangelical, or fundamentalist thing, because none of these names mean anything to God. It's a "we're the body of Christ and we desperately need the Spirit's help right now" thing. As someone said, "Do not be satisfied with ordinary Christianity, but be saying, 'If no one else is heavenly minded, why not I? If others are not full of the Holy Spirit, why not I?'"

Let's ask God for the kind of sensitivity that young Samuel developed in discerning and responding to the leadings of the Spirit. Let's discover more about the Spirit's gifting, fruit, and ways of working so we can become more like Jesus, not by human effort but by the Spirit's enabling. I'm aware that lukewarm churches and faithless theological experts will dismiss this as emotional extremism. The proof will come when God begins to do his mighty redemptive acts among us. We have the Bible and centuries of Holy Spirit-inspired revivals as proof of what God can and will do when we seek him.

**Let's pray that our lives and churches will be focused on Jesus Christ and his gospel.** We all should study anew the New Testament documents to discover our true spiritual heritage. We need more gospel sermons and gospel praise and worship music that glorify Jesus Christ and the salvation he has given us. But we only get that through a careful study of what the good news of Jesus sounds like in its original purity. May God inspire great Jesus-centered preaching from our ministers better than anything Moses or Ezra could have ever preached. May the Lord also give us new music that magnifies Jesus, the cross, and his love for all of us.

Sincere believers in Jesus today are living during a critical hour in the history of Christianity in America. What will we do? How will we respond to the obvious challenge before us? It doesn't matter how young or old you are, how much education you have, or how much talent you possess. Remember what Samuel learned from God when he anointed young David as the future king: "The LORD does not look at the things people look at. People look at the outward appearance, but the LORD looks at the heart" (1 Sam. 16:7).

A Holy Spirit renewal with a return to the New Testament as our authoritative guide is the only hope. We can continue having "church" as is being commonly experienced, or we can have the living Christ. We can hold tightly to our denominational traditions and the way we grew up in church, or we can humble ourselves and ask God for what *could be* rather than *what is*. We can rely on formulas and new clever methods, or we can rely on God's omnipotence to be our source of power.

> **We are living during a critical hour in the history of Christianity in America.... A Holy Spirit renewal with a return to the New Testament as our authoritative guide is the only hope.**

Let us individually pray and ask God for direction and then respond as young Samuel did centuries ago, "Speak, LORD, for your servant is listening."

# Notes

1. http://christianity.about.com/od/denominations/p/christian today.htm
2. John Dickerson, *The Great Evangelical Recession: 6 Factors That Will Crash the American Church ... and How to Prepare* (Grand Rapids: Baker, 2013), 32.
3. http://www.lifeway.com/Article/news – 2012-southern-baptist -annual-church-profile-report
4. https://www.barna.org/congregations/556-what-people-experience-in-churches#.Uh0BRBafvd4
5. Ibid.
6. Ibid.
7. http://www.americanbible.org/uploads/content/State_%20of_ Bible_vert.pdf
8. Ibid.
9. Ibid.
10. http://www.lifeway.com/Article/research-survey-bible-engagement-churchgoer
11. *Weymouth New Testament* (San Antonia, TX: Harrison House, 2012).
12. http://www.intothyword.org/apps/articles/default.asp?articleid=3 6562&columnid=3958
13. Ibid.

# Spirit Rising

## Tapping Into the Power of the Holy Spirit

*Author: Jim Cymbala with Jennifer Schuchmann*

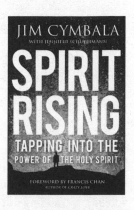

For some of us, being a Christian is harder than it should be. We wonder what happened to the power and the joy that Jesus promised. Jim Cymbala believes that many of us are missing something vital. Christianity for even the best-intentioned person or church, he says, is impossible without the Holy Spirit. You can have regular devotions, great preaching, a strong emphasis on the Bible, and a great worship team, but if you aren't vitally in touch with God's Spirit, you are missing out on the life God has for you.

The Holy Spirit, he points out, is God's agent on earth. Yet he is the least understood, least preached about, and least discussed member of the Trinity. Too often, the body of Christ is divided into two sides. One side stresses the Word of God, separating itself from what it views as the emotional fanaticism often linked to those emphasizing the Holy Spirit. The other side is sometimes known for drifting into unbiblical manifestations and unorthodox teaching while attributing it all to the Spirit of God. But the Christianity we see in Scripture is both grounded in the Word and full of the Spirit.

With stunning stories of how God is working in the lives of people and churches today and with biblical teaching about the Holy Spirit, Jim Cymbala invites you to experience God in a fresh and vital way.

Softcover: 978-0-310-33953-3
Hardcover: 978-0-310-24125-6

*Available in stores and online!*

# You Were Made for More

## The Life You Have, the Life God Wants You to Have

*Jim Cymbala with Dean Merrill*

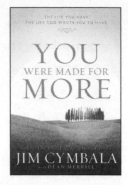

Jim Cymbala knows something a lot of us miss—that a comfortable, secure life won't produce the satisfaction we long for. How could we feel fulfilled by missing out on the life God has for us? Whether or not life seems good right now, Jim Cymbala believes that God has more for you.

In this book he helps you find out how to access the "more" God intends—more peace, real joy, and a deep sense of purpose. As you open yourself to the "more" of God, you will also discover your unique work assignment, the one thing God is calling you—and no one else—to accomplish for the sake of his work in the world. *You Were Made for More* draws a compelling picture of people just like you who are finding that "more of God" means more influence, more energy, and ultimately more happiness. It will help you picture what your own "land of milk and honey" might look like—the fuller, richer spiritual place you long to be. Using examples from the Bible, contemporary stories, and experiences from his own life, Jim Cymbala points the way to a richer, deeper life, helping you take hold of everything God wants to give.

Softcover: 978-0-310-24127-0

*Available in stores and online!*

# Breakthrough Prayer

## The Secret of Receiving What You Need from God

*Jim Cymbala*

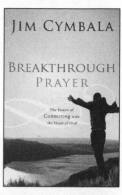

In this book meet three people who discovered the power of "breakthrough prayer."

"My husband and I had a dream of helping desperate young women. But no banker in his right mind would finance such a venture. So we prayed, and God broke through every single obstacle we faced. That was just the beginning of the wonderful roller-coaster ride we call 'faith.'" —Grace (chapter 7)

"Voices inside my head were constantly screaming at me. I became like an animal in the street, muttering or yelling out a stream of profanity as people passed by. One day I screamed out, 'Jesus, help me! O God, you're my only hope!' That was the breakthrough prayer that saved my life." —Danny (chapter 2)

"Talk about breakthrough prayer! I was buried under 110 stories of steel and concrete after the collapse of the World Trade Center Towers when God heard my cry for help." —Genelle (chapter 3)

Softcover: 978-0-310-25518-5

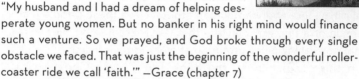

*Available in stores and online!*

# The Life God Blesses

## The Secret of Enjoying God's Favor

*Jim Cymbala with Stephen Sorenson*

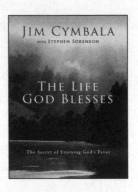

God Is Searching for People to Bless

Jim Cymbala believes that God plays "favorites"—that certain people experience his blessings more abundantly than others. Have these people learned a formula or a simple technique that will guarantee his blessing? Or is there something more profound at work in their lives?

In this companion to the book *The Church God Blesses*, Jim Cymbala points out that God is constantly searching for people to bless. He's not looking for men and women with special talents or unusual intelligence or great strength, but for those who possess a certain kind of heart. Find out how to have a heart that God cannot resist, and you will become a channel of his blessing for your family, your church, and your world.

Softcover: 978-0-310-24202-4

*Available in stores and online!*

# The Church God Blesses

*Jim Cymbala with Stephen Sorenson*

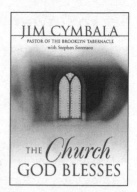

God wants to transform his church into a people of power, joy, and peace. *The Church God Blesses* reminds us that Christianity is only as strong as the local church and that God wants to bless our churches in ways we can't possibly imagine. It doesn't matter whether a church is alive and growing or barely surviving on life support. It doesn't matter whether a church is facing financial challenges, internal divisions, or strife among its leaders. God is able to deal with any problem a church will ever face—as long as his people earnestly seek him.

Cymbala knows that God's blessing and grace is available to us today just as much as it was in the early church, when thousands of people became believers despite the fact that the church lacked everything we consider vital: church buildings, seminaries, printed materials, sound systems, choirs, and money. None of these things mattered. What mattered was that God's hand was on the church, working through his people to build the kingdom. Then, as now, God has chosen the church to manifest his presence to the world.

In this companion book to *The Life God Blesses*, Cymbala describes the kind of church God wants to bless and use. Based on the Word of God and personal experience, *The Church God Blesses* describes the key elements found in a vitally alive church and offers church leaders and individual Christians a fresh and invigorating look at what God intends the church to be.

- Receive solid spiritual nourishment
- Can trust in God's protection
- Engage in vital praise and worship
- Become effective in ministry
- Learn that confession of sin is the channel to God's power

Softcover: 978-0-310-24203-1

# Fresh Power

## What Happens When God Leads and You Follow

*Jim Cymbala with Dean Merrill*

We Need God's Power

Drawing examples from the Bible and from the sidewalks of New York City, *Fresh Power* shows what happens when the Spirit of God moves in our midst. He longs to reveal the mind of God to us and to release heaven's limitless resources to meet the desperate needs around us. *Fresh Power* will expand your vision for what God can and will do, and inspire you to pray like never before for God's power in your church—and in you.

Softcover: 978-0-310-25154-5

*Available in stores and online!*

# Fresh Faith

## What Happens When Real Faith Ignites God's People

*Jim Cymbala with Dean Merrill*

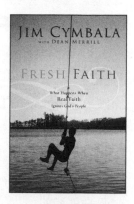

Pastor Jim Cymbala calls us back to a fiery, passionate preoccupation with God that will restore what the enemy has stolen from us: our first love for Jesus, our zeal, our troubled children, our wounded marriages, our broken and divided churches. Born out of the heart and soul of The Brooklyn Tabernacle, the message of *Fresh Faith* is illustrated by true stories of men and women whose lives have been changed through the power of faith. Cymbala writes, "Real faith is produced when our hearts draw near to God himself and receive his promises deep within." That kind of faith can transform your life—starting today, if you choose.

> "Jim Cymbala is an exciting reminder of God's desire to bless and use any faithful and trusting follower of our Lord in supernatural ways."
> —Dr. Bill Bright, the late Founder and President, Campus Crusade for Christ International

Softcover: 978-0-310-25155-2

# Fresh Wind, Fresh Fire

## What Happens When God's Spirit Invades the Hearts of His People

*Jim Cymbala with Dean Merrill*

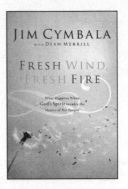

The times are urgent!

God is on the move.

Now is the moment to ask God to ignite his fire in your soul!

Pastor Jim Cymbala believes that Jesus wants to renew his people—to call us back from spiritual deadends, apathy, and lukewarm religion. Cymbala knows the difference firsthand. Forty years ago his own church, the Brooklyn Tabernacle, was a struggling congregation of twenty. Then they began to pray ... God began to move ... street-hardened lives by the hundreds were changed by the love of Christ ... and today they are more than ten thousand strong. The story of what happened to this broken-down church in one of America's toughest neighborhoods points the way to new spiritual vitality in the church and in your own life. *Fresh Wind, Fresh Fire* shows what the Holy Spirit can do when believers get serious about prayer and the gospel. As this compelling book reveals, God moves in life-changing ways when we set aside our own agendas, take him at his word, and listen for his voice.

Softcover: 978-0-310-25153-8